The Six O'Clock Presidency

The Six O'Clock Presidency

A Theory of Presidential Press Relations in the Age of Television

Fredric T. Smoller

PRAEGER

New York
Westport, Connecticut
London

Library of Congress Cataloging-in-Publication Data

Smoller, Fredric T.
    The six o'clock presidency : a theory of presidential press
relations in the age of television / Fredric T. Smoller.
        p.   cm.
    Includes bibliographical references.
    ISBN 0-275-93598-1 (alk. paper)
    1. Television broadcasting of news—United States. 2. Presidents
in the press—United States—History—20th century. 3. Presidents—
United States—Press conferences. 4. Television and politics—
United States—History—20th century.   I. Title.
PN4888.T4S68   1990
070.1'95—dc20   90-31180

Library of Congress Catalog Card Number: 90-31180
ISBN: 0-275-93598-1

First published in 1990

Praeger Publishers, One Madison Avenue, New York, NY 10010
An imprint of Greenwood Publishing Group, Inc.

Printed in the United States of America

∞

The paper used in this book complies with the
Permanent Paper Standard issued by the National
Information Standards Organization (Z39.48-1984).

10 9 8 7 6 5 4 3 2 1

To my mother,
and to the memory of my father and brother

Contents

Illustrations

FIGURES

TABLES

PHOTOGRAPH

Preface

This book attempts to build an empirically based theory of television
network news coverage of the U.S. Presidency. In building this argument I have tried to integrate several of the more important themes discussed in the expanding literature on the U.S. media: the emergence of
television network news as the most important medium in U.S. politics;
the corporate structure which underlies the ownership of the major
media outlets; the impact of technological breakthroughs such as satellite communications, videotape, and mini-cameras; and the emergence of network correspondents and anchors as powerful political
actors in their own right.

The argument advanced in these pages suggests that television news,
the nation's primary source of information about the presidency, may
contribute to the decline and fall of modern presidents. This argument
could conceivably be used to justify the excesses and criminal acts of
past administrations. Some may see this as an attack on this nation's
commitment to a free and independent press. I intend it as neither.
Nevertheless, I believe that citizens must be made aware of the defi-
ciencies in the current relationship between the president and the
most powerful communications medium known to man if that relationship is to advance democratic values.

I am especially grateful to Larry Dodd and Bruce Buchanan for the professional support, intellectual stimulation, and personal friendship they have provided me over the years. Larry Dodd taught me how to build and test theories of contemporary American politics, and the importance of doing so; Bruce Buchanan sparked my interest in the presidency. Thanks also to Woody Kay for suggesting the title, and to Ryan Barilleaux and Erwin Hargrove for reading through the entire manuscript and for providing much needed criticism and thoughtful guidance. Although he writes primarily about Congress, Richard Fenno convinced me that political scientists should, whenever possible, observe the institutions and people they write about first hand—in addition to collecting and analyzing data. Chapman College's Research Council and the American Political Science Association provided me with much needed financial support at various stages of this project. I am especially grateful to my wonderful colleagues in the Social Sciences Department at Chapman, especially to my chairman, Arthur Blaser, for cheering me on when the going got tough, and to my editor, Dana Mildebrath, for punching up my prose. I would also like to thank the good people at CBS, NBC, and ABC news for allowing me to look over their shoulders from time to time. My greatest debt is to my wife, Lidija, without whose love this book would never have been completed.

The Six O'Clock Presidency

1

Television News and the Presidency

French statesman Alexis de Tocqueville made a prophetic observation more than a century ago about the relationship between the presidency and the press:

> The number of periodical or semiperiodical publications in the United States surpasses all belief. The most enlightened Americans attribute the slightness of the power of the press to this incredible dispersion; it is an axiom of political science there that the only way to neutralize the effect of newspapers is to multiply their numbers. . . . With so many combatants, neither discipline or unity of action is possible, and so each fights under its own flag.[1]

He added, "It is not the case that all the political newspapers in the Union are lined up to support or oppose the administration, but they use a hundred different means to attack or defend it. Therefore American papers cannot raise those powerful currents of opinion which sweep away or sweep over the most powerful dikes" (de Tocqueville, 1969:185).

Although de Tocqueville did not foresee TV news, he did anticipate its consequences. Today, the big three networks (ABC, NBC, and CBS) are major actors in U.S. politics. Americans rely on evening news programs as their main source of information about the president (Ranney, 1983).

Consequently, White House aides pay particular attention to how the president is portrayed in those programs (Deaver, 1987).

Most political analysts agree that television has had an enormous impact on the presidency, but there is little agreement about the nature of that impact. Some people feel that television has strengthened the presidency. According to presidency scholar Thomas Cronin, "A president who is knowledgeable in its use can use it to shape public opinion, to gain support for his policies, and to boost his chances for political survival. . . . Television fixes on a president and makes him the prime symbolic agent of government" (1980:95–96). Some media watchers believe television news actually became an extension of the Reagan White House. *New York Times* reporter Steven Weisman (1984) and ABC News White House correspondent Sam Donaldson (1987) point to the controls placed on the press by President Ronald Reagan's staff. No modern president, for example, has held fewer press conferences, kept the press at a greater distance, or stage-managed presidential events more brilliantly. Those efforts resulted in favorable coverage of the president and his policies. Such coverage, it seems reasonable to assume, contributed to Reagan's tremendous popularity.

Others suggest that the balance of power between the president and the press has shifted decidedly in favor of the press. Reporters, in this view, have become too cynical and overly critical of presidential activities and policies and, since Vietnam and Watergate, have leaned harder on the president and his staff (Moynihan, 1975; Jordan, 1982; Powell, 1984). Television news brought the Vietnam War, Watergate, the pardoning of Richard Nixon, the Iranian hostage crisis, and the Iranian-Contra affair into the nation's living rooms and thereby contributed to the collapse of the Johnson and Nixon administrations, the electoral defeats of Gerald Ford and Jimmy Carter, and the weakening of the Reagan administration. Such coverage has made it increasingly difficult for televised presidents to govern (Ranney, 1983). Reagan White House aide David Gergen has said, "I question whether the George Washingtons and Ben Franklins and Thomas Jeffersons could have survived as popular figures under the klieg lights of national television" (1982:11).

Speculations about the actual content of TV news coverage of the president have not been subject to extensive empirical examination over the course of several administrations. This study examines 5,292 presidential news stories aired on the "CBS Evening News" from January 20, 1969, to January 20, 1985. The Nixon, Ford, and Carter administrations and the first term of the Reagan administration were included in the sample.[2]

The programs were not viewed directly; instead, the verbatim microfiche transcripts prepared by CBS were read and coded. The sample included news stories concerning the president's daily activities, his foreign and domestic policies, and his personal life. These stories were coded for type of activity portrayed, duration or length, rank in the broadcast, and source and substance of criticisms made of each administration. The stories were also coded according to their portrayal of the president, his policies, and his administration—favorable, unfavorable, or neutral. Stories with a balance of favorable and unfavorable were coded neutral. Starting from the presumption of neutrality, the question was asked: Is this story favorable or unfavorable to the president? Since the study was interested in the casual viewer's first impression of a story, a rather flexible coding scheme was used (see Appendix A). Briefly, this is what was found:

- Television news is obsessed with the presidency. One fifth of a typical "CBS Evening News" broadcast contained stories about presidential policies and activities.
- While the bulk of the coverage is neutral, the majority of directional (positive or negative) coverage is negative—an unfavorable balance overall.
- Television news is getting "tougher" on the presidency. Each full-term administration president since Richard Nixon has received a bigger measure of poor coverage than his predecessor.
- The tone of the coverage the president receives appears to be correlated with his Gallup support rating.

THE "MIRROR" METAPHOR

How can these results be explained? To find out, I spent several weeks with the White House press corps during spring 1982 and summer 1986. I observed the press at work in the pressroom in the White House and on the road and conducted interviews with television news executives, correspondents, and technicians for ABC, CBS, and NBC as well as White House officials (see Appendix B).

The answer I repeatedly was told was the same one media analyst Edward Epstein received when he researched his classic *News from Nowhere* (1973a). "Television news," several correspondents and news executives told me, "was like a mirror." It simply reflects presidential policies and performance.

Presidents are the most important political actors in U.S. politics, so it is natural that they receive a lot of coverage by the media. Much of that coverage is inherently negative because a troubled economy, changes in the international political balance of power, and increased (and conflicting) expectations by voters have made the presidency an increasingly difficult—if not impossible—job (Barger, 1984).

While "reality"—concrete presidential actions and statements and events that transpire during the course of a presidential term—is the most important determinant of evening news coverage of the White House, media analysts and news professionals readily concede that a two-minute story cannot begin to mirror the complexity of the modern presidency. Listen to former White House correspondent Dan Rather:

> There is no way that . . . [a] . . . White House correspondent . . . can come out there in a minute and 15 seconds and give the viewer even the essence, never mind the details or the substance [of a president's policies] . . . . One of the great difficulties with television is that it has a great deal of trouble dealing with any subject in depth.[3]

If Dan Rather is correct, how then does the image of the presidency that appears in the nightly network broadcasts differ from reality? In short, how does the medium shape the message? This book provides an answer to that question.

First, this book will argue that the content of the news is shaped by the medium of television itself. In the case of the presidency, a network's political, commercial, and technical needs produce a bias toward *extensive* and *negative* coverage. By *extensive coverage* I mean that the president receives far more coverage than journalistic or academic values suggest that he should receive (Buchanan, 1987). By *negative coverage* I mean that the tone of the bulk of the coverage a president receives after his first six months in office is unfavorable. New technologies have made it easier for the networks to lavish attention on the presidency. In addition, the advent of celebrity correspondents and anchors, who are less intimidated by the president and his staff, and increased competition among the networks have reinforced the tendency for negative coverage. Second, in addition to being extensive and negative, news coverage of the president is also *thematic*. Producers and correspondents integrate their daily coverage into ongoing themes that provide dramatic unity over a prolonged period of time. The use of ongoing themes means that correspondents and producers do not have to explain the background of a particular story each time they report on it. While there are many long-running stories about the president, there is one theme that tends to dominate. It takes the form of the question, How well is the president doing? Over the course of an administration, the networks provide four different answers. I refer to this transformation in the content and tone of White House reporting as the "four seasons of presidential news."

The four seasons proceed as follows: First, during the initial months of a new administration, network news profiles the new president and his appointees and those close to him. Later the press shifts its attention to the politics and substance of the president's legislative program. In the third season, the networks' need for new and original news items about the president leads to a premature evaluation of his policies. In the final season, the president himself is reevaluated. In short, the president is profiled; then his policies are examined. These policies are evaluated, and then the president is reevaluated.

The nature of televised press coverage of the president has created a dilemma for modern presidents. Left unchecked, television's portrayal of the president, as described here, will lead to the erosion of public support. However, efforts by the White House to combat television's portrayal of the president by managing news coverage (e.g., by keeping reporters from the president, by not taking questions on subjects it does not wish to address, or by giving misleading, distorted, or dishonest answers to reporters' queries) will subvert democratic values.

This collection of observations about the economics, technology, and personnel of network news is called *The Six O'clock Presidency* because its origins reflect the needs of the commercial networks (e.g., the need to be visually interesting and entertaining) as opposed to the values implicit in the Constitution (e.g., the need for citizens in a democracy to have access to the information necessary for them to evaluate the president and his policies).

The six o'clock presidency is worthy of extended discussion for several reasons. First, loss of public support undercuts the president's ability to govern. Public approval influences the reception the president's proposals receive in Congress, his clout with foreign and domestic elites, his ability to influence key members of the bureaucracy in charge of implementing his domestic agenda, and the boundaries of his constitutional power. In addition, a president's approval rating has been shown to be a good predictor of the vote share received by incumbent presidents running for reelection and of the success members of the president's party encounter in midterm elections.[4]

Second, the six o'clock presidency has had a profound impact on the organization and operation of the White House. So powerful and pervasive is the impact of television that the White House has remade itself in television's image, along the lines of evening news' needs. Network needs influence the timing and nature of virtually all the president's activities (e.g., Reagan held his press conferences after the evening news programs were concluded so that gaffes or misstatements would not be the focus of the networks' coverage). Recent administrations have devoted increasing resources to public relations efforts that have been aimed mainly at television news. High-level aides and the president himself also appear to spend an inordinate amount of time on image-making and image-enhancing activities, with the result being less time spent on substantive matters (Deaver, 1987; Regan, 1988).

Finally, because it is unlikely that network policy concerning coverage of the presidency will undergo fundamental change in the near future, it is probable that future presidents will become increasingly isolated from the press and that efforts by the White House to manage the news (e.g., by moving reporters out of the White House pressroom or by circumventing the press altogether by setting up their own White House news channel) will increase. Such actions have important implications for democracy: Presidents are increasingly isolated from the people through their representatives in the press, and citizens are deprived of information that is crucial to their evaluation of the president's performance in office.

One final note: The six o'clock presidency is a subtle phenomenon. Despite extensive interviews, on-site observations, and an extensive data base, it will undoubtedly be impossible to prove the entire argument. The argument presented here suggests that the networks are not out to get the president. (There is, for example, no "bias" group or committee or management structure that dictates policy at any network. The argument presented here says that extensive negative news reporting of the presidency is a natural by-product of television news and its needs. It is doubtful that interviews with members of the press or any analysis of the operational policy structure of any of the major television networks would uncover a conspiracy to topple the current or past administrations.) *Presidential decline is an unintended consequence of the judgments that influence the gathering and editing of the news.*

The organizational routines of network news influence U.S. politics in a manner comparable with the influence exerted by the Constitution or the laws that govern the electoral process; these influences are subtle, long term, and wide in scope. But unlike those formal legal documents, the dynamics of network news are invisible to each newly elected administration, which believes that it can successfully control the press. And these dynamics are only partially revealed to the networks, who believe that their coverage is fair, unbiased, and as accurate as they can make it.

The six o'clock presidency is rooted in the ways in which four groups of actors involved in the gathering and production of presidential news go about their jobs. Chapter 2 presents these actors. Chapter 3 discusses the built-in incentives that encourage the networks to lavish attention on the presidency. Chapter 4 discusses the rules that define how news content is to be presented and how they bias coverage of the president in a negative direction. These procedures are reinforced by the changes in the correspondents who cover the White House for the networks. Chapter 5 presents the procedures used to explore the six o'clock presidency and the results of the analysis of the "CBS Evening News" transcripts. Chapter 6 suggests how press coverage varies over the course of a presidential term. Chapters 7 and 8 consider how Presidents Carter and Reagan responded to the six o'clock presidency and the consequences of their media strategies. Finally, Chapter 9 explores possible reforms in the relationship between the presidency and the press.

NOTES

1. De Tocqueville (1969:184–5).
2. Chapter 5 contains the procedures used in the selection of the sample and the coding of the data.
3. Dan Rather, as quoted in Purvis (1976).
4. See, for example, Edwards (1983:8–37).

2

The Four Environments of Presidential News

Decisions concerning news coverage of the president are made at four levels by four groups of actors: (1) by Washington reporters, primarily those at the White House; (2) by the Washington bureau, primarily the assignment editor and the news producer assigned to the story; (3) by the president of CBS News and his assistants in the CBS News New York office, and (4) by company executives, such as CBS's new owner Laurence Tisch. Each group is distinguished by its goals, working environment, and decision processes.[1] The relationship between these four groups can be viewed as a series of concentric circles (see Figure 2.1).

Each of these four groups exercises independent influence over a distinguishable aspect of presidential news. At the center are the Washington-based correspondents, primarily those who are assigned to the White House; also included are those whose reporting touches on the presidency and administration policies (e.g., correspondents who cover Capitol Hill or the State Department). Of the decision makers examined, correspondents have the most discretion on a daily basis over the content and tone of presidential news.

The next ring represents the Washington bureau, to whom chief Washington correspondents are directly responsible. The bureau coordinates the activities of the correspondents, technicians, producers, and editors of each story.

Figure 2.1
The Four Environments of Presidential News

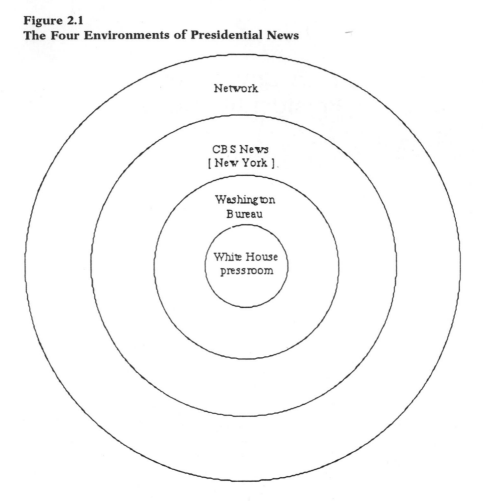

The next environment examined is the CBS New York newsroom. There, senior producers and the managing editor decide which stories go into the evening newscast, their length, and their order. Producers must cull from the dozens of stories available the lineup for that evening's show. By doing so, they determine the amount of news coverage given to the president.

The fourth and final level is the network. Network executives such as founder William Paley or current owner Laurence Tisch generally do not interfere in the day-to-day functioning of CBS News. Their influence is more subtle and long term. It becomes apparent, for example, in decisions concerning the news division's budget. For example, recent cutbacks have meant that CBS News has not been able to cover domestic and particularly foreign news stories as comprehensively as it once did (Rather, 1987).

A chain of command clearly exists between these four groups of decision makers. Correspondents are constrained by the decisions of the Washington bureau chief; the Washington bureau chief is constrained by the CBS News New York office, which in turn is constrained by network policies. The network itself is constrained by legal, political, and economic forces in the external environment.

GOALS

The Columbia Broadcasting System is a large and lucrative Fortune 500 corporation whose first and foremost concern is profit. The profit motive pervades the entire organization. As anchor Dan Rather notes, "More profits. That's what business is about. News is a business. It always has been. Journalists understand and accept that" (Rather, 1987:25). The strategies for pursuing increased profits vary by environmental context.

The network enhances profit by maintaining corporate prestige. The news division works to increase profits by keeping costs down while simultaneously keeping ratings high. Producers in the Washington bureau use technical pizzazz to widen the network's audience share. White House correspondents, in part, generate conflict that attracts viewers by confronting White House officials. Let us examine these environments in greater detail.

Network

Network executives work in a highly political arena and must be judicious in the pursuit of profits. Certain types of news activities (specifically those that violate Federal Communications Commission [FCC] rules or disgruntle the opinion of the public, powerful elites, or special-interest groups) can jeopardize profits by alienating viewers and affiliates or by inducing new federal regulations of lawsuits. Network executives, such as CBS founder William Paley, appreciated television's power to influence U.S. politics and culture. His steadfast commitment to the news division and its commitment to the presidency enhanced the corporation's prestige. Paley, ever an astute businessman, understood that if television was to forestall government regulation, and therefore clear the way for increased profits, it must earn some minimal level of respect from governing elites and opinion leaders. News coverage of the political process, with the presidency as its focal point, was a means to that end.

News Division

CBS News is a division of the Columbia Broadcasting System. Head-quartered in New York City, it has its own president and executive staff and is responsible for the network's various news programs. The "CBS Evening News," which is produced in New York and reaches approximately 14.5 million viewers, is its most important broadcast.[2] The New York office coordinates the activities of its domestic and foreign bureaus and closely monitors them. All scripts must be cleared by the New York producers, who are also frequently the source of story ideas. Producers in New York regularly consult with producers concerning how stories will be covered.

Executives at the CBS News division, such as CBS News president Howard Stringer, clearly work within a *commercial*, not political, arena. It is their job to keep costs down and rating up. These are the measures that will be used to evaluate their performance because low ratings may mean that the network will lose affiliates or advertising revenues—or both.

Washington Bureau

The Washington bureau is not directly concerned with corporate profits or "CBS Evening News" ratings—although it will be affected by a downturn in either area (e.g., through layoffs or personnel and format changes). Instead, producers have one main objective: to make the news "look" good. Technical pizzazz is the name of the game.

Producers showcase their talents through the creative use of visuals and graphics, or by getting good pictures from a difficult site—all while meeting tough deadlines. They must be sure that each story conforms to the technical quality and policy guidelines set down by the network, but they also want to dazzle their peers in the Washington broadcast community. According to CBS News producer Susan Zirinsky:

> There is a real big mandate for pieces to not be boring—no standup, no bland-looking stuff. CBS News wants it to be more visually enticing. So you try to be more creative. People are not going to watch if it is just a standup. And polls show that viewers like what we are doing, which is pepping up the news.

White House Pressroom

Reporters who cover the president on a regular basis work in the West Wing of the White House. The main briefing room has 48 seats for the approximately 100 reporters who cover the president on a daily basis. At the front is a small stage with a podium bearing the presidential seal. A blue curtain, which provides the contrast television cameras require, forms a backdrop. This is where the press secretary holds briefings and where the president holds "mini" press conferences. Television cameras are set up on a platform at the back. Correspondents can "go live" from the briefing room, as well as from others parts of the White House, by plugging into cables that link them to the Washington bureau.

A short corridor connects the briefing room to a second room where there are rows of cubicles for print reporters. Each of the networks has a booth not much bigger than a walk-in closet in the back of this room. Inside, there is a counter with typewriters, a television set, and several phones—little else. CBS assigns four reporters and two technical crews (a sound person and a camera person) to the White House each day, twice as many as it does to Congress. All three networks commit more money and personnel to White House coverage than they do to any other beat.

The atmosphere of the pressroom is very informal. Technicians are dressed in jeans; electronic equipment crowds the aisle; light chatter fills the air. A table in an adjoining lunchroom is often the site of a card game. It is not unusual to see a technician or reporter napping or reading the paper.

Coverage of the White House differs vastly between print and electronic media. Obviously, a White House correspondent must accurately record what the president says and does. However, since Vietnam and Watergate, most print reporters have felt the need to go beyond the official White House story. Reputations for journalistic excellence, such as those earned by the *New York Times* and *Washington Post*, have been built through time-consuming, in-depth stories as well as forceful and eloquent writing.

The networks, however, rarely conduct in-depth reports on the White House. Instead, each has relied on its most visible correspondent to go "toe to toe" with the president and his aides. Such confrontations generate viewer interest and reinforce the network's image as democracy's "watchdog"—but often without the substance found in print. Thus, Sam Donaldson (1987:4) writes that it is his job "to challenge the president, challenge him to explain policy, justify decisions, defend mistakes, reveal intentions for the future, and comment on a host of matters about which his views are of general concern."

Table 2.1
Source of Coverage

Actor	Context	Goal	Coverage
Company	Political	Reduce Uncertainty	Extensive
News Division	Commercial	High Ratings	Extensive
Washington Bureau	Technical	Pizzazz	Extensive/Negative
White House	Journalistic	Confrontation	Extensive/Negative

To summarize, the six o'clock presidency is rooted in decisions made by these four groups of individuals: CBS network executives, senior producers in the CBS News New York office, the Washington bureau, and Washington reporters (see Table 2.1). Policies made at all four levels result in a commitment by the networks to cover the president extensively. News judgment decisions made in the Washington bureau and the White House contribute to a negative portrayal. The next two chapters will show how.

NOTES

1. My strategy for exploring these environments borrows heavily from Richard Fenno's work on congressional committees. See Fenno (1973).

2. Between September 19, 1988, and January 15, 1989, the number of people two years old and over who tuned into the "CBS Evening News" was estimated by CBS News to be 14.5 million.

3

The Scope of White House News

Photo opportunities, briefings, releases, more photo-opportunities. Most of it doesn't mean a damn thing. But the White House grinds it out and we eat it up. The network wants everything we can give them on the president.

Ed Bradley,
CBS News Correspondent

I mean, I have to argue not to be on "World News Tonight" some nights, because I don't think I have a story. Whereas many of my colleagues (not covering the president) at ABC are desperately trying to get on.

Sam Donaldson,
ABC News Correspondent[1]

On a lonely peak, high in the Santa Barbara mountains, two men monitor a screen wired to a camera attached to a giant lens. Some 3 feet long and 16 inches wide and weighing more than 400 pounds, it is one of the largest camera lenses ever made. It was built specifically to watch a small house three miles in the distance.

The men are technicians for CBS News. Their assignment is always the same: Get good pictures of the president of the United States while he is vacationing at his ranch.

The technicians leave their oceanfront hotel at six in the morning.

Photograph 3.1
Giant Lens

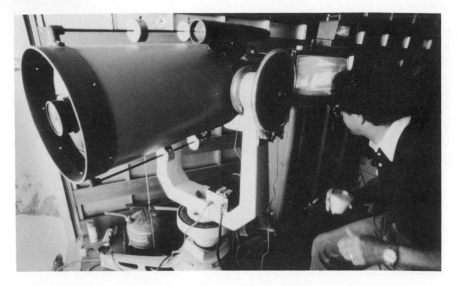

A technician, using a giant lens, observes President Reagan's vacation house outside of Santa Barbara from "privacy peak." Photo by Steve Malone.

The daily trip up the narrow and winding road to "privacy peak" takes over an hour. The final climb is so steep and so rutted that it must be made by foot or with a four-wheel-drive vehicle. The lens is so big and expensive that it remains at the top of the mountain in the back of an enclosed truck under 24-hour guard.

The crew's day is spent waiting for the president to do something—ride his horse, clear brush, take a walk. The hours pass. Finally, the president comes out for his daily ride. The crew snaps into action and captures the man as he passes through their lens.

The White House knows the networks crave pictures of the president. They also believe that the American people want, perhaps need, to see their president on television fairly regularly. The president rides out so that the cameramen can get their footage. Mission completed, the technicians radio to their producer. A decision is made whether the vigil should end for the day. (The president may come out later to clear brush!)

Those pictures of President Ronald Reagan's horseback ride were not cheap. The technicians' salaries, the lens, the truck, and the 24-hour guard add up to a fairly substantial investment for a piece of tape that will run several seconds and is of dubious news value. No speeches were made, no policies were enacted, and no shake-ups in the govern-

ment were announced; nothing of any real significance took place—
just the president going for a ride on his horse Little Man.

Most presidential news is not this trivial. Nevertheless, the image of
this enormous lens peering at the president from so great a distance,
and its presence on the mountaintop involving great effort and substantial cost, illustrates television news' obsession with the presidency,
as well as the way in which technology has made the satisfaction of that
obsession possible. Television devotes considerably more resources to
the presidency than to any other continuing news story (Grossman and
Kumar, 1981:259). All media pay special attention to the presidency,
but no medium pays more attention than television (Robinson and
Sheehan 1983:191).

Why so much presidential news? Network executives I spoke with
said that the president is inherently newsworthy and therefore deserving of the amount of coverage he receives. The president, they said, is
the symbolic leader of the nation, the center of governmental action,
and the only nationally elected policymaker in U.S. government. In the
nuclear age, the president is, quite simply, the single most important
person in the world. Moreover, since Vietnam and Watergate, many reporters have viewed the presidency as a potential threat to democracy.
As democracy's watchdogs, they feel it is their job to critically evaluate
the president's performance on a daily basis.

But there are six additional, less grand, reasons why the networks
lavish so much attention on the presidency:

1. News coverage of the president is profitable because information
   about the president sells.
2. By focusing on the presidency the networks are able to deliver to their
   affiliates a "national" news program that does not compete with local
   news programs.
3. White House news helps fulfill the FCC's requirement that broadcasters serve the public interest. Proximity to the president elevates network prestige.
4. White House news is cost-effective.
5. White House news is logistically easy to produce.
6. Airtime also advances the careers of correspondents assigned to the
   White House.

This analysis suggests that extensive coverage of the president satisfies organization imperatives and that television news covers the president for reasons other than the fact that he is inherently newsworthy.
These imperatives are found in each of the four environments pre-

sented in the previous chapter. This chapter examines those incentives and other related concerns.

THE PROFIT IMPERATIVE

The Columbia Broadcasting System (CBS) is a big Fortune 500 corporation whose first and foremost concern is profit. The network makes money by selling advertising time in its programs. To maximize profits, the network tries to maximize the audience share its news programs receive by reporting on people and events that are of interest to the broadest possible range of viewers.

Thus, the primary reason the networks provide far-reaching coverage of the president is because they are in the news and entertainment business, and snazzily packaged information about the president sells.[2]

Citizens have always been interested in the affairs of the presidency, but television has made it possible to satisfy that demand on an unprecedented scale. This demand is reflected by the explosion in news coverage of the president by all media during the 1970s and 1980s. Only 15 reporters, for example, were present when Harry Truman announced that a nuclear bomb was being dropped on Japan. Today, approximately 1,800 reporters hold press passes to the White House pressroom.

A concern for profits, however, is not the only reason the networks cover the president. Network newscasts do not cover Hollywood personalities or sports on a regular basis even though these topics are in demand. There are additional incentives—unique to the presidency—that reinforce this commitment.

NETWORK

The Affiliate Imperative

Media analyst Edward Epstein pointed out in *News from Nowhere* (1973a) that the network's relationship with its affiliates also affects the content of the evening news. The number of people who watch a program partly depends on the number of affiliates who carry that program. By law, each network can own only a handful of television stations.[3] So in addition to its own stations, the network contracts with approximately 200 independently owned affiliates across the country to carry programs. This allows the network to deliver a national audience to sponsors and to charge accordingly. Local stations receive a percentage of that advertising dollar. They also get network programs (programs that they do not have the resources to produce) as well as the right to sell advertising time in some of those programs. The rub is, if a local station refuses to carry a program (and by law this is their decision to make), the network cannot reach that affiliate's market. That is why it is critical for the network to remain on good terms with the affiliates. One of the ways it does this is by producing a qualitatively different program (Epstein, 1973a:103). Thus, local news focuses on local news, sports, and weather, and the network focuses on international and "national news."

One problem the network faces is that virtually all news is local news for some affiliate. The closing of a steel mill in Pittsburgh is going to be covered by the Pittsburgh affiliate and is probably only of interest to that community. But a story about the influx of Japanese products—a trend that is of interest to the entire nation—might show pictures of that same steel plant along with pictures of new Toyotas being unloaded from a ship onto a dock in Long Beach, California, and Sony videocassette recorders being sold in New York City. This is called "nationalizing" the news.

The need for national news is a strong incentive for the networks to lavish attention on national political institutions. But the Supreme Court is tough for the network to cover because it does not allow televised coverage of its proceedings. It is also hard for the network to get a handle on Congress, with its dispersed committee system, weak leadership, deliberative nature, and 535 locally elected members. As former White House correspondent Robert Pierpoint said, "A great deal of news comes down off Capitol Hill, much more than the White House, but it is channeled individually to the congressman's or senator's home area because it is not always national news. And that is very important to keep in mind, because most of the reporters who cover the Congress cover it for individual states or districts." So the networks focus their cameras on the only political official who is elected by the entire nation. Explains CBS News vice president John Lane, "We are in the business of supplying national news, and whatever the president says or does is by definition national news."

The Political Imperative

Affiliates also influence evening news content because it is they, technically speaking, not the network, who are licensed by the FCC. In practice, however, the networks are bound by the same set of rules because each owns local stations. Up until 1983 the FCC required that stations "serve the public interest" by contributing to the "development of an informed public opinion through the public dissemination of news and ideas concerning the vital public issues of the day" (Epstein, 1973a:48).

The "quiz show" scandals of the 1950s, however, cast doubt on television's commitment to "serve the public interest." In order to increase their ratings, contestants to game shows "Twenty One" and "$64,000 Question" were given partial answers to the questions before the show. The increased ratings that resulted—viewers like to watch people win rather than lose—more than made up for the prize money awarded. Polls taken shortly after scandal broke found that television's credibility had been seriously damaged. Industry leaders realized television needed to regain lost respect if it was to increase its profits, compete effectively with newspapers, and ward off further attempts at government regulation (Robinson, 1977:9). They turned to news, and particularly to coverage of John Kennedy (of his presidency and his assassination), as a palpable example of their commitment to the public good.

Kennedy was one of the first politicians to recognize television's potential to influence public opinion. He was a Catholic, relatively inexperienced, and a rich man's son who won the presidency by a very slim margin. He used television to broaden his appeal and to establish his competence as a political leader. On several occasions he used television to explain his domestic and foreign policies, most notably after the Bay of Pigs debacle. He also permitted the networks to film his press conferences live, thus enhancing the status of the reporters who appeared on camera with him.

Kennedy was bright, handsome, articulate, witty, and urbane—he and his family made "good television." Television introduced the nation to the First Family. Mrs. Kennedy guided the public on a televised tour of the White House. Now, not only had Kennedy come into our homes; we were going through his as well. Television reinforced the psychological bond between the people and the president.

Television coverage of the Kennedy assassination firmly established television news' credibility and secured its place in U.S. society. It was Walter Cronkite, Chet Huntley, and David Brinkley—not Lyndon Johnson or any other political leader—who comforted the nation. It was television news anchors—not congressional leaders or Supreme Court justices—who were credited with providing a steadying influence during this period of national crisis. And it was television news that helped legitimize the transfer of power to a vice president in whose home state the president was murdered. Within a week, television news became indispensable to the presidency and to the nation. Today, when critics attack the networks' prime-time offerings, network executives can point with pride to the news division and the critical role it plays as overseer of U.S. politics.

NEWS DIVISION

The Budget Imperative

There are strong incentives for the cost-conscious "CBS Evening News" producer to use Washington stories, particularly news stories from the White House. First, the transmission of Washington news stories to New York is not charged against the division's budget—as are coaxial or satellite transmissions from other areas. CBS, for example, paid $10,000 to get a single taped report out of Iran during the hostage crisis (Boyer, 1988:90). Second, White House costs are fixed; the correspondents, technicians, and necessary equipment are in place, generating stories and pictures; the "protective coverage" (discussed below) generates yards of videotape that is available to each network for free; and direct communication (via microwave or coaxial cable) with the pressroom is possible 24 hours a day. No advance ordering of satellites or coaxial lines is necessary. Former White House correspondent Robert Pierpoint put it this way to me:

> As a producer putting together an evening news show, you can always take a story from the White House, and it will sound like news whether it is or it is not. You can depend on White House news. And when you are a producer putting together a news show for 15 million Americans every night, you want to be sure that you are going to have enough stories for that night's broadcast. But if you are facing court decisions that may not come down in time or satellites that are broken or unavailable, or if your correspondent trying to get from the Beirut airport to the transmission point doesn't make it, you are in deep trouble. But you always know that you can get a piece from the White House that looks and sounds like news.

WASHINGTON BUREAU

The Technical Imperative

The logistics involved in television reporting are quite complicated and expensive. Television news teams need knowledge of an event before it occurs ("lead time") to assign personnel, to truck in and activate equipment, to "order up" satellite and coaxial lines for the transmission of video signals, and to edit videotape.

Advances in mass communications technology have allowed for a more extensive and intensive chronicling of administration activities. Pioneered by the networks, these innovations have encouraged other organizations to cover the presidency, thus swelling the ranks of the press corps. In this way, the networks have become victims of their own commitment to extensive coverage of the presidency. The advent of 3/4 inch videotape and the mini-camera and the availability of satellites for the transmission of video signals are part of the electronics revolution that occurred in television news during the mid-1970s.

The switch to videotape coupled with the advent of the hand-held mini-cam, introduced in the final days of the Nixon administration, lengthened the news day at the White House. (The networks had completed their switch from film to videotape by the end of 1976.)

Film differs from videotape in several key respects. Film needs to be developed; videotape is available immediately for live broadcast. Film is spliced together by hand, a time-consuming and laborious process; videotape is edited electronically, which allows for greater creativity. Portable editing machines make it possible to produce a piece for the evening news virtually anywhere in the world. Moreover, video signals can be transmitted via telephone, microwave, or satellite. Film must be physically delivered. Finally, videotape's pictures are far more vivid than film.

According to several cameramen I spoke with at the White House, in the days of film the news day at the White House tended to end by mid- or late afternoon because several hours were needed for processing and editing the day's coverage. With video, crews can now shoot to within half an hour of airtime, frequently less. Most "stand-ups" (the concluding remarks given by the correspondent) are taped shortly before the program airs. Seasoned correspondents do these live. This allows the reporter to polish his script and present the latest version of a story.[4]

The mini-camera was introduced during the Senate Watergate hearings. Coaxial lines carried its signals directly to the bureau, making live broadcasts from the White House much easier. When the network crews were still shooting film, live broadcasts required that studio cameras be brought in and that semitrucks be parked in the small lot between the White House and the Executive Office Building. Because of the difficulties involved, press secretaries and network producers tended to discourage live coverage unless an event was especially newsworthy. According to Raymond L. Scherer, former network news White House correspondent for NBC, who covered the White House in the 1960s, press secretaries were reluctant to displace their coworkers from their coveted parking spaces.

Tape's increased clarity also allows the networks to take full advantage of the various telegenic "sets" at the White House, such as the splendid Rose Garden, the ornate East Room, and the White House lawn, with the stately presidential mansion in the background. This also holds for images around the world when the president goes abroad. These pictures, regardless of the content of the story being reported, make for good television.

Finally, the mini-camera and the use of videotape made *protective coverage* (or *the body watch*) much easier. As the term implies, the networks, on a rotating basis, videotape every step the president takes outside the White House. Such coverage was limited during the 1960s because it was often difficult and always expensive to find remote facilities to process film. So it seemed wasteful to record every moment of John Kennedy's motorcade through Dallas; that is why the only moving pictures of the assassination available to the press were shot by a private citizen.

That fall, CBS and the other network news organizations learned an important lesson: The president must be covered whenever there is a possibility, no matter how remote, that he may be hurt or injured. This means that every step that the president takes that can be videotaped is taped. Former NBC News White House correspondent Judy Woodruff (1982:11) explains how the body watch worked on March 30, 1981, the day John Hinckley shot President Reagan.

> We . . . monitor every step the President takes to the extent that the [Secret] Service permits. . . . In addition to the pool reporter and crew, who are responsible for coverage of the President from the moment he leaves the White House until he arrives at his destination, each network typically assigns one or possibly two of its crews. The day of Ronald Reagan's speech at the Hilton, NBC set up one crew near where the President's limousine would park, in order to videotape him from the instant he emerged from the hotel door at which point the pool was supposed to take over. Inside the ballroom where the President was to speak, a second crew was ready to begin rolling as soon as he entered the room and throughout his speech. . . . A third roving NBC crew was also present this day to photograph the president for the documentary in progress.

The accessibility of satellite transmission in the 1970s also facilitated television coverage of the presidency. Before videotape and satellite transmission became available, film had to be flown or mailed to New York, resulting in significant delays, especially when the president was

overseas. Satellites allow for the instant transmission of signals from almost anywhere in the world.

   Videotape, mini-cameras, and communications satellites made covering the president easier and more cost-effective for the networks.
Technological breakthroughs, particularly the mini-cam's relatively
low cost and ease of use, were powerful incentives for independent and
local stations from across the United States and around the world to
join the White House press corps.

WHITE HOUSE PRESSROOM

The Career Imperative

   Correspondents compete aggressively to get their stories included in
the 22-minute evening news broadcast because airtime is an important
measure of success in television news, critical to career maintenance
and advancement (Gates, 1978). Thus, Leslie Stahl told me:

> Sometimes the White House hasn't given me anything and I haven't
> thought of anything, but I really want to be on the air—and I do, face it.
> So I start making calls and I call people in the White House, in the admin-
> istration, in the Congress, and friends I know from way back. And I even
> call my father. And I just sort of say, "What do you think?" And sometimes
> they say, "You ought to do a story on blah, blah, blah." Or a guy on Capitol
> Hill will say, "Have you heard about the memo?" or "Have you seen the
> letter?" or "Do you know what is going on with this?" or "Have you heard
> what they have done with that?" or whatever.

   The White House is a high-profile assignment, so the networks put
the most preferred correspondents there. As a result, naturally they
have a much better opportunity to get on the air. The belief here is that
viewers like to see familiar faces. So the network tries to build up a following for what Peter Boyer calls the "A-List" of correspondents by
using them on a regular basis (Boyer, 1988: 123–124). Most important,
White House correspondents are under substantial pressure to produce presidential news to justify the networks' commitment. ABC
White House correspondent Sam Donaldson (1987:196–97) illustrates
how this can lead to coverage of dubious news value.

> Now, mind you, in a perfect world I could report back to New York that
> there wasn't any news on Guadeloupe and all the reporters, producers,
> technicians, couriers, and hangers-on sent there at great expense could

go out for another swim. This is not yet that perfect world, however, and I knew we had to report something and probably at the top of our news broadcast. [Pierre Salinger] discovered the private residence where the leader would dine that night. He learned the menu. Roast pig. Not only that, he had persuaded the host to let ABC News come by for an exclusive look at the oven in which the pig would be roasted .... NBC and CBS were beaten that night by an exclusive report on the roasting of the presidential pig.

CONCLUSION

This chapter has suggested several of the needs that influence the presentation of presidential news. Extensive coverage allows the network to present a national news program to its affiliates. Proximity to the president elevates network prestige. The president provides a "peg" around which to discuss U.S. politics and American society in relation to other political institutions, nations, and cultures. The presidency is a fairly convenient and cost-efficient device for explaining U.S. politics to the American people. The networks are able to increase ratings and profits by organizing much of their political coverage around the activities and fortunes of the president.

Extensive coverage by itself, however, would not give rise to the dynamic that characterizes network news coverage of the president. It must be accompanied by negative coverage. The next chapter will delve into some of the organizational imperatives that lead to a negative portrayal of the president.

NOTES

1. Both quotations are from Robinson (1983:191).

2. The networks are not the first to recognize the marketing potential of the U.S. presidency. During the latter part of the nineteenth century, U.S. newspapers became major businesses. In order to attract large advertising accounts, newspapers increased their circulation by featuring items about the president. As George Juergens (1981:6–7) points out:

[One] consequence of the new journalism was increased stress on human-interest material, in reporting on government as well as in other areas. Newspapers had to respond to the reality that by and large readers are more interested in personal details about figures in the news than in dry matters of statecraft. The wisdom applied above all in the case of the president of the United States. Scandal and gossip about chief executives had always been grist for the press, but now what can only be described as a kind of domestic chatter became a staple of White House reporting.

3. In 1984 this number was increased from 7 to 12. See Hertsgaard (1988:181–2).

4. Interestingly, Sam Donaldson told me that he prefers to do his stand-up live or within minutes of airtime, which involves greater risk because additional takes are not possible if he flubs his lines. But it also reduces the editorial discretion ("script clearance") of the correspondent's superiors since no time is permitted for the previewing of the correspondent's closing remarks.

4

The Negative Bias of
Network News

For producers and reporters, bad news is good news.
>   Irving R. Levine,
>   NBC News[1]

A good editor in this or any other newsroom would much rather
embarrass the President than make him look good.
>   Robert Kaiser,
>   *Washington Post*[2]

As the above quotations illustrate, news by its very nature is negative.
Television, like print, defines news as the departure from the norm.
News organizations do not cover the safe arrival of a jet or the Missis-
sippi flowing peacefully to the Gulf; crews rush to crashes and floods.
Grossman and Kumar (1981:35) are right when they describe what
news organizations want from their White House reporters:

What their news organizations want most are interesting stories about
what the President is going to do, preferably before they become common property. They want their stories filled with illuminating details
about individuals whose stars are rising and stories about those who are
on the decline. Especially when the President's troubles are reflected in a
decline in the polls or in defiant opposition from interest groups, Congress, the Bureaucracy, and the private sector, correspondents seek to in-

clude embarrassing items about the kinds of deals White House officials have made or are about to make, blunders committed by the President and his staff in their relations with key people or groups, and contradictions between a President's words and his actions.

But television's coverage of U.S. politics is more negative than print because competition among the networks, production values (among them a desire for pizzazz), and the aggressiveness of White House network correspondents provide an extra negative "spin" (Robinson and Sheehan, 1983). This chapter focuses on the competitive pressures and format constraints producers in the Washington bureau face each afternoon as they put together the White House spot for the Dan Rather news. The latter part of this chapter focuses on the emboldenment of the network correspondent.

WASHINGTON BUREAU

Decisions concerning news coverage and the implementation of network policies are made in the Washington bureau. This is where presidential news stories are built and where the limitations imposed by the nature of the medium are accommodated. The need for pictures and assumptions about the nature of the viewing audience systematically influence television news coverage of the president.

The Visual Imperative

Television news needs good pictures to compete with other news media. The problem with pictures is that they condense, simplify, and exaggerate political phenomena; so politics is often portrayed in "black and white," "good and evil" terms. (The "grays," the qualifications and nuances of political activities, are lost.)

Like political cartoons, news pictures are effective devices for symbolic communication (which is why television is ideally suited to political campaigning). So when presidents or candidates control media access, they have a formidable political tool at their disposal. But because pictures present complex political phenomena in symbolic terms, reality is often exaggerated.

According to Rex Granum, Atlanta bureau chief for ABC's "World News Tonight" (and a former deputy White House press secretary during the Carter administration):

Basically, when things aren't going well at the White House, the evening news' portrayal is worse than in fact the reality is. And then when things are going well for an administration, the stories suggest that things are far better than they are. There is a tendency to extremes because television is so dependent on pictures. The Camp David peace agreement between Israel and Egypt is a good example. Those pictures of Carter and Begin and Sadat embracing are just wonderful visuals. The impression they leave is that what occurred was 100 percent positive. A newspaper reporter, however, might go on for two thirds of his story about what a great achievement it was. But might for the last third talk about the history of the problem and certainly how insurmountable it has been up to this point. He might also add that this achievement hasn't been as great as it may appear. A negative example would be hecklers at an event who threw tomatoes at the president. This is so visually compelling that the resulting story will be a one-minute spot that says: "Yes, the president spoke, but he was heckled throughout, and following his speech the crowd threw three tomatoes." The visuals of the tomatoes splattering on the secret service agent would be the lasting impression that you would come away with. It would have to be arguably ten times more dramatic to come across in print. So in print you would talk about what was said in the speech and so forth, that he was heckled throughout, and then three tomatoes were thrown.

The need for interesting pictures reinforces journalism's penchant for the unusual. So network news coverage of presidential faux pas and clumsiness—visually compelling but often gratuitous, trivial, and unrepresentative stories—receive more coverage than they might otherwise merit *solely because of their value in pictures.*

ABC White House correspondent Sam Donaldson (1987:191) illustrates the point:

[Reagan went to the Vatican] in 1982, during a European trip that had been overscheduled, leaving him, and us, insufficient time to rest. So he seized the opportunity to take a nap during his audience with the pope. As the president sat under the hot television lights listening to Pope John Paul II's welcome, Reagan fought to stay awake. He lost. Our cameras zeroed in, and that night we showed the presidential nap. Not only did we show it that night, we have shown it again and again and again because all the interesting, even ghastly, scenes of presidential deeds and misdeeds go into the tape library, where they are instantly available for recall and reuse.

Videotape is often edited so as to intensify the activity being reported by focusing on those scenes with the most action (Edwards, 1983:147). So a 30-second piece of tape of Gerald Ford walking, stumbling briefly, and then resuming his pace would likely be edited to a much shorter piece that focused just on the stumble. The result: a story that portrayed Ford as a far less competent president than he really was. Does it matter? Former President Gerald Ford (1979:289) thinks so:

> Every time I stumbled or bumped my head or fell in the snow, reporters zeroed in on that to the exclusion of almost everything else. The news coverage was harmful. . . . [This] helped create the impression of me as a stumbler. And that wasn't funny.

Television's voracious appetite for good pictures makes it necessary to highlight those aspects of the presidency that are amenable to pictures and ignores those that are not. It encourages coverage of conflict, controversy, and other melodramatic events rather than the plain, routine functioning of government. Says Susan Zirinski, a producer for the "CBS Evening News":

> I covered President Reagan when he went to Pittsburgh. There were the angriest demonstrators in the two years that I have been traveling with him. However, if I just had the two crews that was the normal standard on the road I couldn't have gotten good pictures of those demonstrators. I had another crew sent in from New York just to cover them, and that became the main focus of the story.

Finally, there are aspects of the presidency that simply cannot be photographed (Nessen, 1980). Actions (like a bill signing or a presidential tour of a nuclear power plant) receive more attention and have greater impact than processes (such as the development of policy options, negotiations, or the evolution of ideas). The power, purpose, and functioning of the office is systematically exaggerated and distorted.

For example, President Carter's efforts to get the U.S. hostages in Iran released could not be shown in pictures. Instead, descriptions of the president's actions had to compete with visually and emotionally engrossing pictures of angry Iranian students burning the U.S. flag. Presidential actions such as the ordering of troops on a mission to free the hostages will receive more coverage than stories concerning the evolution of that policy decision or, more important, the constraints that inhibit the exercise of presidential power.

Television transmits a simple surface impression, whereas national policy issues are infinitely complex and many-sided. "The ugliness of military combat or economic deprivation can be graphically conveyed in a few pictures and sounds; the complex policy considerations that usually lie behind a decision to risk these consequences are much more difficult to explain" (Cutler, 1984:118).

The Entertainment Imperative

News coverage of the president is also greatly influenced by network policies that assume that viewers have a very limited attention span. If viewers are presented with an "uninteresting" report, they can simply flip the channel; so producers have developed a variety of conventions for keeping viewers tuned in.

Stories are kept short and simple, usually no more than 90 seconds. According to Atlanta bureau chief for "World News Tonight" Rex Granum, "You don't go on the air with only two pieces, which is what you are talking about if you are talking about more complex stories. You just don't do business that way. You have 10 or 11 or 12 pieces. If you put two pieces on, pretty soon the executive producer is going to be out of work because nobody is going to watch the show." This means that the complexity of the presidency is rarely captured in news reports. Who would know better than Walter Cronkite?

> Inadvertent and perhaps inevitable distortion ... results [from] the hyper-compression we all are forced to exert to fit one hundred pounds of news into the one-pound sack that we are given to fill each night. ... Our abbreviated versions of the news are suspect. ... We fall far short of presenting all, or even a goodly part, of the news each day that a citizen would need to intelligently exercise his franchise in this democracy. So as he depends more and more on us, presumably the depth of knowledge of the average man diminishes. This can clearly lead to disaster in democracy. [Barrett, 1978]

Producers keep their reports entertaining (and superficial) by employing symbols and by personalizing their presentations. Familiar images and themes maintain viewer interest.

> Gas pumps, supermarket checkout lines, and school buses, for example, are shown to represent the issues of energy, inflation, and civil rights, respectively. Complex issues are presented in terms of human experience. Easily recognizable symbols encourage people to project themselves into the story, but they may not contribute toward edifying them. At other times stories are personalized through using experts, spokesmen, or random representatives of groups (poor or unemployed persons, for example). [Edwards, 1983:147]

The Melodramatic Imperative

Finally, producers model individual reports along the lines of the "narrative form" instead of the "inverted pyramid," popular in traditional print. Reports that follow the inverted pyramid format present the most important information first; the least important is presented last.

Television, on the other hand, tells stories. According to NBC News president Reuven Frank, "Every news story should, without any sacrifice of probity or responsibility, display the attributes of fiction, of drama. It should have structure and conflict, problem and denouement, rising action and falling action, a beginning, a middle, and an end."[3]

The narrative format reinforces television's simplistic, abbreviated, and truncated portrayal of the president. Reports are cast as minidramas or melodramas. The primary objective, as in a soap opera, is to entertain, not to inform.[4] Correspondents are forced to define complicated issues and vague personalities sharply. So presidents and presidential candidates are portrayed as stereotypes—The Hatchet Man, The Klutz, The Incompetent, The Great Communicator, and The Wimp. Such shorthand is used in newspapers, too, but it is particularly prevalent in television news.

The narrative format also accentuates reporting of conflict within the administration and between the administration and other political actors (such as Congress, interest groups, and foreign governments such as the Soviet Union or Libya). The president is portrayed as a "winner" or "loser" when his legislation is considered on Capitol Hill or the effects of his foreign policies are being assessed. Conflict between the White House and other political actors (like the press, the State Department, big business) is often portrayed in "hero" and "villain" terms.

Herbert Stein, an economic adviser in the Nixon administration, argues that the narrative format distorts the president's handling of economic problems.

> This tendency to dramatize and personalize is particularly evident in the explanations the media routinely give for the problems of the economy. These problems have a long and complex history; they involve not just one nation but all nations, in varying degrees, at any one time; and they have no simple, single cause. The economic "story" requires a villain and a straight plot. . . . For many years the villain was Nixon; then for a while, it was the Nixon holdovers; now it is more simply the administration. In each case the crime was the failure to provide "leadership." The content of this leadership was rarely spelled out. [H. Stein, 1975:40]

When a president is successful (that is, when his programs are being passed by Congress and critics have not yet emerged) during the initial months of a new administration, this can work in his favor. But later, when the president is more moderately—or simply less—successful, the tendency of television news to dramatize reality to attract viewers increases the president's negative portrayal.

The Problem

Inherent in the very nature and organization of television news are imperatives that exert a subtle but persistent, cumulative, and mutually reinforcing bias to a negative portrayal of the president:

1. The length of the evening news requires stories to be short and un-complicated. This contributes to an abbreviated and simplistic portrayal of the president.
2. The need for pictures causes television news to exaggerate and distort the functioning of the presidency by emphasizing those aspects of the presidency that are amenable to pictures.
3. The need for good visuals reinforces journalism's definition of the news as the departure from the norm, which often leads to unfavorable coverage.

These tendencies are reinforced by assumptions about the nature of the viewing audience that focus and intensify coverage of conflict within the administration and between the administration and other political actors.

So, on one hand, we have a complex and multifaceted office that is based on persuasion and the subtle exercise of power and influence. An office in which most significant activities are conducted in private. An institution with limited formal power that must struggle to reach and maintain consensus. An institution in which the execution of routine governing chores is offered as one measure of competence. And an institution that depends on public support for success.

On the other hand we have a medium that requires simplistic, visible indicators of presidential performance. A medium that is ideally suited to the portrayal of conflict. And a medium whose purpose is to cover the unusual and atypical.

The result of these conflicting needs? The organization imperatives faced by the news bureau predispose it toward a negative portrayal of the presidency. This tendency is reinforced by changes that have occurred in the White House pressroom.

THE WHITE HOUSE PRESSROOM

During summer 1941 a story went around Washington that British officials were running up huge restaurant, telephone, and bar bills and charging them to Franklin Roosevelt's cherished Lend-Lease program. Under the headline "British Here Make Whoopee as U.S. Pays," a Washington *Times-Herald* story claimed that the British actually sang a song (to the tune of "There'll Always Be An England") that went: "There'll always be a dollar, as long as we are here." A follow-up story by New York *Daily News* reporter John O'Donnell suggested that Lend-Lease funds were being used for drums of rum, sherry, port, and brandy glasses.

At a news conference on August 5, 1941, Roosevelt "snapped [O'Donnell's] head off" and condemned the reports, calling them "vicious rumors, distortion of facts, [and] just plain dirty falsehoods" ("Lie of the Week," 1941:10). Sullen and taken back by this bitter outburst, the reporters turned to another topic. The press conference proceeded like any other. On another occasion, Roosevelt was so upset by O'Donnell's reporting that he once awarded him a mock Nazi iron cross for stories that he felt were unpatriotic (Tebbel and Watts, 1985:450). Reporters he found irritating and disagreeable were assigned to his "Dunce Cap Club."[5]

Some 33 years later, during the final stages of Watergate, at a National Association of Broadcasters convention in Houston, CBS White House correspondent Dan Rather rose to ask President Richard Nixon a question. Talk of impeachment was now being taken seriously, and the president was traveling the country to bolster support for his beleaguered administration. Rather was intensely disliked by the president and his staff, who felt his reports were unfair, politically biased, and unduly harsh. *New York Magazine* referred to him as "The Reporter the White House Hates."

As Rather rose to his feet, the audience of TV executives applauded. Many also booed. President Nixon, surprised and agitated by the audience's reaction, remarked, "Are you running for something?" Rather snapped, "No, sir, Mr. President, are you?" The president stared intensely at Rather and did not respond (Rather, 1977:18).

These two confrontations illustrate an unmistakable trend in Washington politics in the postwar era: Reporters have become much more aggressive and contentious. Why the change?

The frequently cited reason is that a profound change occurred in the media during the 1960s and 1970s. Most reporters supported the New Deal and an activist president. They were also united in their desire to defeat Germany and Japan. Vietnam and Watergate, however, taught the press that presidents are fallible and will lie if necessary to cover their mistakes. As democracy's watchdogs, many reporters feel it is their job to protect the nation from abuse of power by the president and other high government officials. As Bob Woodward of the *Washington Post* has said, "You have to remember that our experience for the past ten or fifteen years has been that in the end the government official always ended up being guilt as charged. We just didn't run across people whose defense held up under close scrutiny (Powell, 1984:173).

THE EMBOLDENMENT OF THE TELEVISION CORRESPONDENT

Not only have the attitudes of the media toward the presidency changed; so, too, have the men and women who cover the president.

Washington has always attracted the nation's best and brightest journalists. However, pretelevised presidents had an intellectual and social edge over reporters. Roosevelt, for example, was from one of the nation's most prominent families, he graduated from Harvard, and although he hardly needed it, his official salary was $75,000 a year. The press people he faced, Leo Rosten tells us in his 1937 survey, were not nearly as well pedigreed. Most were from middle-class families. Only half graduated from college. Their average salary was $6,000. The highest paid reporter in Rosten's survey earned $25,000, only a third of what the president made (Rosten, 1937).

Prior to television, White House reporters were not widely known outside journalism circles. Today, network correspondents are celebrities whose names and faces are known throughout the U.S. At $25,000 in advertising revenue a rating point, management has a stake in their correspondents' fame. As in local news, the networks vie for ratings by touting their anchors and correspondents. (For example, it is "The CBS Evening News with Dan Rather," "NBC Nightly News with Tom Brokaw," and "World News Tonight with Peter Jennings.") Favored correspondents receive a disproportionate share of high-profile assignments. They are also prominently featured in publicity for the evening news programs and upcoming specials (Boyer, 1988). Realizing that airtime is critical to advancement, many correspondents have minimum levels guaranteed in their contracts (Gates, 1978).

Correspondents look and sound different than the rest of the press corps. As a group, they are more physically attractive. They are taller, better dressed, and better looking. Their voices are generally more distinct. The Ed Asner character "Lou Grant" would never get a job as a network correspondent. As Douglass Cater has written:

It was easier before the age of the anchor to tell who was a journalist and who was a politician. The politician wore a better suit and less rundown shoes. His coiffeur was more impressive, even in a time when men did not admit the services of hair stylists. Nowadays, we witness the transmogrification of Ted Koppel's hair even as Gary Hart's appears to be going back to bush. [Cater, 1986:15]

Correspondents and anchors have all the trappings of star status. Salaries negotiated by theatrical agents generally exceed a half a million—more than twice the president's official salary of $200,000 (Boyer, 1988:250; *The World Almanac and Book of Facts*, 1989). Salaries exceeding a million for the most prominent correspondents are not uncommon. Network news anchors are among the most well paid people in society. Anchor Dan Rather makes $3 million a year (Boyer, 1988:255). As in Hollywood, attention is lavished on appearance; voice, wardrobe, and performance coaches assist in the development of a desirable on-air persona. It is not uncommon for news personalities to be driven to work and to be pampered and fawned over by attendants once they arrive (Blair, 1988).

When traveling with the president, correspondents are booked in the best rooms in the finest hotels, away from the rest of the corps, who receive less lavish accommodations. Several have written books about their experiences at the White House (Dan Rather, *The Camera Never Blinks* [1977]; Judy Woodruff, *This Is Judy Woodruff at the White House* [1982]; Sam Donaldson, *Hold On, Mr. President!* [1987] and have made the rounds of the talk-show circuit to boost sales. One of Sam Donaldson's chapters is titled "Fame."

The White House also fusses over them. Correspondents are seated in the front row of the pressroom and in the first-class section of the press plane. The best positions on camera platforms are also reserved for network correspondents and crews. They are generally the first ones ushered to and from a presidential event by White House staffers.

Network correspondents are not just rich and famous; they are also powerful. By power, I mean they have the ability to significantly influence the nation's future. For example, during the 1960s, Walter Cronkite became one of the most trusted and respected persons in the U.S. in a decade when many had lost faith in national leaders and political institutions. No single political leader was as effective in ending the Vietnam War as was Walter Cronkite. David Halberstam wrote, "It was the first time in history a war had been declared over by an anchorman" (Halberstam, 1979:716). In 1977, Cronkite played a major role in arranging Anwar Sadat's historic trip to Israel. Cronkite had heard talk that the Egyptian president was willing to travel to Israel. Cronkite, in a taped telephone conversation that CBS broadcast, asked Sadat if indeed he was willing to go to Israel. To Cronkite's surprise, Sadat said he was willing to go at any time. Cronkite then called Israel's Menachem Begin and told him of Sadat's comment. Shortly thereafter, the Israeli prime minister sent an invitation to Sadat to visit the Jewish state. ("Television's Blinding Power," 1987:20). No congressman or senator or Supreme Court justice ever retired with the national fanfare that

Cronkite received when he left the "CBS Evening News" in 1981 (Gates, 1978:208–24).

So as yesterday's news hounds have become today's show dogs—as they have become richer, more famous, and more powerful—they have become more confident and therefore more willing to challenge the president and his staff. There are many important exceptions, but as a rule television correspondents are less cowed by the president and his staff than the press corps. Driven by an intense desire to scoop the competition (in this case, NBC and ABC) and perhaps a psychological need to justify their high salaries, and by a need to prove themselves to their peers in print, correspondents dominate the pressroom, press conferences, the daily press briefing, and virtually every other White House–press interaction, often to the consternation of their colleagues in print. As CBS's Bill Plante said to me, "We [the network correspondents] are perfectly aware of the low esteem with which we are held by the other reporters around here."

Before television, no reporter dared ask a president to defend himself against charges that his "administration is inept," as Sam Donaldson did of Jimmy Carter, or to comment on the perception that "disarray is here in the White House, that you have been out of touch, that you have had to be dragged back by your staff and friends on Capitol Hill to make realistic decisions on the budget," as Donaldson did of Ronald Reagan (Donaldson, 1987:4).[6] Before television, reporters never spoke to White House officials as Dan Rather did to George Bush, then the vice president and the Republican party's presidential nominee: "Mr. Vice President, you've made us hypocrites in the face of the world. How could you, how could you sign on to such a policy" ("Bushwacked,"1988:17). Such confrontations generate the sparks that many viewers find engaging.

Finally, recent changes in the industry have reinforced the negative bias in broadcast news that this chapter has detailed.

CHANGES IN THE BROADCASTING INDUSTRY

During the 1980s the three networks' dominance of national and international coverage came to an end. For the first time, the number of viewers who tuned in to their news broadcasts and prime-time programs declined. In the 1979–80 TV season, the three network news shows reached 76 percent of the TV viewing households; by the 1986–87 season, their share had fallen to 62 percent ("The Way It Is for the Network News," 1987). Millions of dollars in potential advertising revenue were lost. The decline is attributed to the proliferation of cable television news shows (e.g., CNN, "MacNeil-Lehrer News Hour," and

C-Span) and a drop in the cost of transmitting video by satellite, which allowed local stations direct access to national and international news stories. Cable and the popularity of the videocassette recorder also eroded the network audience share for its prime-time programs.

The drop in viewers boosted competition among the news divisions of each of the networks. Unprecedented pressure was applied by new owners at all three networks to increase profits.[7] Journalistic values were pitted against business and entertainment values as never before. According to television news insiders, business and entertainment values won (Rather, 1987). CBS Bill Moyers put it this way in a 1986 *Newsweek* interview:

> At CBS the line between news and show business has traditionally been there, and the people in charge have tried to protect news against the intrusion of entertainment values. . . . Managers defended the news division against outside aggressors (Jesse Helms and Ted Turner) but yielded to the encroachment of entertainment values from within. Not only were those values invited in, they were exalted. The line between entertainment and news was steadily blurred. Our center of gravity shifted from the standards and practices of the news business to show business. In meeting after meeting, "Entertainment Tonight" was touted as the model—breezy, entertaining, undemanding. In meeting after meeting the discussion was about "moments"—visual images containing a high emotional quotient that are passed on to the viewer unfiltered and unexamined. ["Taking CBS News to Task," 1986: p. 53.]

CONCLUSION

The previous chapter demonstrated how economic and political concerns in all four environments led the network to a policy of extensive coverage. This chapter has shown how organization imperatives within the Washington bureau predispose it toward a negative portrayal of the president. This tendency is reinforced by changes that have occurred in the White House pressroom. Now the question arises, Are these assertions true? Let us turn to an examination of the data to find out.

NOTES

1. As quoted in D'Souza (1986:28).
2. As quoted in Hertsgaard (1988:91).
3. As quoted in Epstein (1973b:41). The evolution of the narrative form is provocatively discussed in Schudson (1982:97–112); see also William Henry

III, "News as Entertainment: The Search for Dramatic Unity," in Abel (1981:133–58).

4.   The term *melodramatic imperative* is used by Paul H. Weaver (1976:6ff.).

5.   Interview with James Roosevelt, the president's son. The "Dunce Cap Club" is referred to in Roosevelt's 660th press conference, July 12, 1940. See the *Complete Presidential Press Conferences of Franklin Roosevelt* (1940, vols. 15–16).

6.   Sam Donaldson is also a regular guest on the Sunday morning program "This Week with David Brinkley," where he regularly provides his opinions concerning the president and his policies.

7.   During this time, each of the networks received new owners. Capitol Cities Communications merged with ABC; General Electric acquired NBC; and Loews' Corporation, headed by financier Laurence Tisch, purchased CBS. New managers cut the news divisions' budgets; laid off correspondents, technicians, and other personnel; closed bureaus; and cut back on national and international news.

5

Exploring the Six O'Clock Presidency

The previous chapters presented reasons for extensive negative reporting of the presidency by television network news. This chapter asks, Is this in fact the case?

To explore the nature of television news coverage of the presidency, I read and coded the transcripts of 5,292 presidential news stories that were aired on the weekday "CBS Evening News" from January 20, 1969, through January 20, 1985. The Nixon, Ford, and Carter presidencies and the first Reagan administration were included in the sample. The programs were not viewed directly, however. Instead, the verbatim microfiche transcripts prepared by CBS were used. The sample included news stories concerning the president's daily activities, his foreign and domestic policies, and his personal life. These stories were coded for the type of activity portrayed, story tone, length, and rank.[1] Commentaries by Eric Sevareid and Bill Moyers were coded but were not included in the analysis of news stories.

SAMPLING DESIGN

A computer program was used to develop a stratified random sample of 1,800 weekdays. The sample had to be large enough so it would be amenable to extensive analysis but small enough so it would be manageable by a single researcher. Based on a small sampling of stories, it was estimated that there are approximately three presidential news stories per day. Thus, a sample of 1,800 days would produce approximately 5,400 news stories.

The population of the sample consists of the 4,180 weekdays in the 16-year period under examination.[2] Thus, 43 percent of the population was included in the sample (1,800/4,180 = .43), a figure that is well above sample sizes typically used in studies of this sort.[3] On average, then, the evening news was examined on predetermined weekdays, two days each week for each of the 832 weeks in the study.[4]

The sample was also stratified by day of the week to ensure that variations in the number and percentage of weekdays (that is, Mondays, Tuesdays, etc.) were kept to a minimum. It has been suggested that news content is biased toward certain days of the week. For example, Mondays tend to include news reports on the discussion or analysis of economic statistics that were released the previous Friday or over the weekend. If the sample had a disproportionately high percentage of Mondays, the number of economic news stories could conceivably be overrepresented in the sample. The tone of news stories in the aggregate could conceivably have a negative bias because of the poor economy during many of the years considered.[5]

INCLUSION DEFINITION

Once the sample of random days was generated, a decision had to be made on a definition of *presidential news*. News stories that met the following criteria were included in the analysis:

All news stories that referred directly to the president, either by name or to his office, were included in the analysis. Thus, coverage of congressional actions that included specific references to presidential reactions was included. Also included were stories concerning the president's family, friends, White House staff, and foreign and domestic policies. On the other hand, executive department stories that did not refer specifically to the president in the story were excluded from the analysis. Also excluded were (1) stories about a remote "presidential task force" or commission that had only a tangential relationship to the president and that were not discussed directly in terms of the president's policies and (2) network announcements of news coverage of the president or related programming—for example, "CBS will present a special on President Reagan's first year in office tonight at 10 P.M."

UNIT OF ANALYSIS

The unit of analysis is the individual report. Stories were conveniently demarcated on a "rundown" sheet that preceded each transcript. Thus, elaborate decision rules concerning where a story began and ended were not necessary. By counting the number and order of stories on the rundown sheet, one could also ascertain a story's "rank" in the broadcast. Likewise, story length was determined by counting the lines of the report.

CODING OF THE TRANSCRIPTS

Each of the stories was coded on the basis of content and tone. Because the tone variable is of crucial importance to the study's findings, it merits separate attention. The stories were coded according to their portrayal of the president, his policies, and his administration—favorable, unfavorable, or neutral. Stories with a balance of favorable and unfavorable were coded neutral. Starting from the presumption of neutrality, the question was asked, Is this story favorable or unfavorable to the president? Since I was interested in the casual viewers' first impression of a story, a rather flexible coding scheme was used. Appendix A contains examples of positive, neutral, and negative stories.

RELIABILITY

Because coding news stories is such a tedious task, it is possible that the coding definitions would not be consistently applied throughout the course of the study. To guard against this, a proscribed set of coding procedures was rigidly adhered to. Coding was done four days of the week (Monday, Tuesday, Thursday, and Friday). All the presidential stories appearing in 25 sample days were coded during each coding session. On average, about five hours a day was spent on coding. It took 72 days to code all the data. Because the stories were fairly short and uniform, they were not difficult to classify.

To check the reliability of the coding procedures, a volunteer was asked to code a randomly selected set of stories from each administration on the basis of tone. The two coders were in agreement 88 percent of the time. This percentage compares favorably with other research of this kind (Grossman and Kumar, 1981; Robinson and Sheehan, 1983).

LIMITATIONS

CBS was chosen over ABC and NBC simply because it is the only net-work for which transcripts are publicly available. During the period considered, CBS also had the most stable format, with Walter Cronkite and then Dan Rather as anchors, and it consistently reached more viewers than did ABC or NBC. The "CBS Evening News" with Walter Cronkite moved passed NBC News in fall 1967 and has remained the highest-rated evening news broadcast ever since (Gates, 1978:444).

Whether the results are generalizable to ABC and NBC is a research question that this study does not directly address. Some analysts feel that CBS was tougher on the White House than either ABC or NBC. Weisman (1983), for example, analyzed a week's coverage of the White House by the big three networks and found that CBS aired more nega-tive reports than either ABC or NBC. White House officials spoken with tended to agree that CBS was the toughest of the three networks in its coverage of the Reagan presidency. (Indeed, this may be precisely why CBS is the ratings leader.) Nevertheless, because the norms that guide the gathering and editing of news, and the types of men and women who report the news, are fairly consistent across the three networks— the factors that this study argues are responsible for extensive negative coverage—there is reason to believe the results are generalizable to NBC and ABC.

Another limitation of this research is that visuals were not coded. This is a criticism that has been made of other analyses of television network news (Adams and Schreibman, 1978). The goal of this content analysis was to examine the largest number of stories across the long-est time frame possible. Although videotapes of the networks' evening news programs are available through the Vanderbilt Television News Archives, their coding would have required commitments of time and resources that were not available.

Finally, the most thorough test of the thesis would be to consider the portrayal of *all* "televised" administrations—that is, Kennedy through Reagan. Unfortunately, a full set of transcripts prior to January 1969 is not available. Therefore, only three of the presidents in the sample (Nixon, Carter, and Reagan) completed a full four-year term. Neverthe-less, this sample of presidents is a diverse one: The presidents exam-ined differ in personality, party affiliation, and ideology. Most important, they achieved different levels of success while in office. The establishment of patterns of news coverage across such widely diverse presidents would constitute partial empirical support for the six o'clock presidency thesis. With these caveats in mind, let us turn to an analysis of the data.

SIXTEEN YEARS OF PRESIDENTIAL NEWS

Extensive Coverage

Does CBS lavish attention on the president? Yes. Of the 1,800 days examined, 97 percent (1,746) had at least one president news story. Furthermore, the majority of the 48 days that contained no presidential news followed an incumbent losing reelection, when the press's attention turns to the president-elect. Between two and three news stories about the president were broadcast on an average evening. Producers spoken with suggested that a typical evening news program airs between 12 and 15 reports. This means that, on average, 20 percent of a typical program is made up of presidential news.[6] Another way of looking at this is to divide the average number of lines of a presidential story into the average number of lines in a typical broadcast. The average length of a presidential news story is 66 lines.[7] The mean length of an evening news broadcast is 350 lines. Again, approximately 20 percent (18.5) of a typical evening news program was devoted to news about the president. This pattern held up in each of the years examined (Figure 5.1).[8]

Although there is no objective benchmark, the devotion of one fifth of a broadcast to one institution is sizable and is interpreted here as being extensive.

Extensive coverage by itself, however, does not undermine presidents. Chapter 4 showed how organizationally based imperatives in two environments (the Washington bureau and the White House pressroom) led to negative news coverage of the president. What do the data say?

Negative Coverage

The results show that 60 percent of the presidential stories aired during the period considered were neutral in tone (Table 5.1). The relatively high level of neutral stories is due to a couple of factors. First, a substantial portion of presidential news is the routine coverage of the office. Stories about presidential appointments and nominations and White House statements tend to have no evaluative dimension, yet they make up a great deal of White House coverage. Second, the conventions of modern journalism require news reports to be balanced, fair, and free from personal bias. Stories that contained a balance of positive and negative comments were coded neutral.

Figure 5.1
CBS Covers the President Extensively

Average Number of News Stories

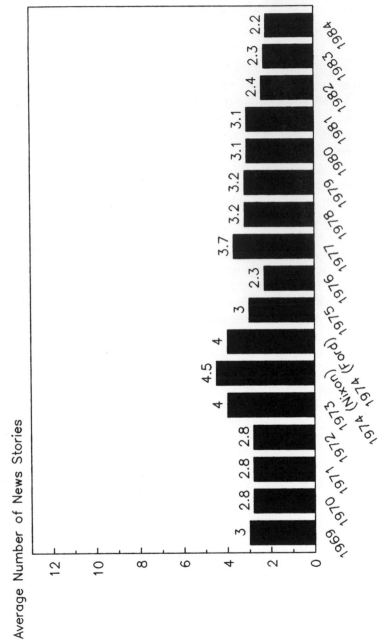

Year

Table 5.1
CBS Is Getting Tougher on the White House

Admin.	Positive	Neutral	Negative	Net Tone
Nixon (1)	24	55	21	+3
Nixon (2)	10	58	32	-22
Ford	19	63	18	+1
Carter	16	59	25	-9
Reagan	11	63	26	-15
Total	16	60	24	-8

Of the remaining presidential stories, 24 percent were negative in tone, and 16 percent were positive. While this 8 percent differential may not appear substantial, keep in mind that negative coverage frequently has much greater impact on public opinion than positive coverage. "Microchanges" in story tone can have "macroeffects" on public support for the president when 45 million people are watching. According to media analysts Martha Kumar and Michael Grossman, "Ten stories about the president's polish and suavity in handling foreign diplomats may pale into oblivion in the face of one story about a major faux pas" (Kumar and Grossman, 1982:86).

Net Tone

Patterns of coverage within and across administrations are significant. The percentage of negative stories subtracted from the percentage of positive stories yields the measure of *net tone*. An example illustrates how this measure was computed: Suppose the evening news one night contained four stories about the president, and the first two were positive, the second was neutral, and the third story was negative. The net tone is the number of positive stories minus the number of negative stories. Thus, in this example the net tone was +1, and the net presentation of the president that evening would have been positive. This measure allows us to capture the *net image* of the president portrayed on the evening news for a given period of time. For example, the net tone for the entire sample was −8. This means that the net evaluative portrayal of the presidents studied was negative. This measure assumes that neutral stories have no evaluative impact on public opinion. It also assumes that positive news stories and negative news

Table 5.2
Net Tone by Year of Study (percentages)

	Positive	Neutral	Negative	Net Tone
Nixon (first term)				
1969	27	54	19	+8
1970	19	60	22	-3
1971	24	54	22	+2
1972	24	53	23	+1
Nixon (second term)				
1973	10	57	33	-23
1974	11	58	31	-20
Ford				
1974	31	54	16	+15
1975	15	68	17	-2
1976	18	60	22	-4
Carter				
1977	25	57	19	+6
1978	15	63	23	-8
1979	11	66	23	-12
1980	13	52	35	-22
Reagan				
1981	18	59	24	-6
1982	8	63	29	-21
1983	6	70	24	-18
1984	13	63	24	-11

stories in effect cancel one another. This admittedly crude measure allows us to capture the *net evaluative image* of the president portrayed on the evening news over time.[9] It is particularly useful when examining how the image of the president portrayed on television news varies within and across presidential terms.

Data from this study reveal that network news coverage of the president is getting increasingly negative (see Table 5.1; also see Table 5.2

and Figure 5.2). Each of the presidents received more negative coverage than his predecessor.

In only 4.5 of the 16 years studied (1969, 1971, 1972, 1977, and Ford's
half of 1974) did the incumbent receive a net positive portrayal (Table
5.2 and Figure 5.2). Nixon received a negative net portrayal for 3 years
of his 5.5-year tenure; net tone scores for 2 of Ford's approximately 2.5-
year presidency were negative; and Carter received a negative score for
3 of his 4 years in office. Contrary to the popular impression that the
networks were cowed by the Reagan administration (Hertsgaard,
1988), "The Great Communicator" received negative scores for each of
his first four years as president. Ronald Reagan (first term) received
more negative coverage by CBS News than any other president, with
the exception of Richard Nixon's second "Watergate" term. (How and
why the president remained so popular despite this coverage is considered in Chapter 8.)

I also found that each full-term president—Nixon, Carter, and
Reagan—had a tougher first year than his predecessor. Nixon's net
tone score for his first year in office was 8; Carter, 6; and Reagan, −6.
Honeymoons (defined here as January 20 through June 30 of the president's first year) also became less enjoyable for each president. Honeymoon periods (Figure 5.3) ended more abruptly and decisively for each
president. Nixon's net tone during his honeymoon was 17; Ford, 13;
Carter, 17; and Reagan, 14. Following his first half year in office,
Nixon's net tone score dropped 9 points; Ford, 15; Carter, 28; and
Reagan, 40 (Figure 5.3). No president since Richard Nixon (first term)
has received a net positive portrayal on the evening news after his first
half year in office.

Content of Presidential News

How can this increase in negative coverage within and across administrations be explained? Has there been a change in the content or tone
(or both) of presidential news? Is the network covering more negative
subjects (like scandals, coded here under the heading "Administrative
Politics") or the same subjects more negatively?

The answer seems to be a little bit of both. I divided the stories into
eight categories (also see Figure 5.4):

- *Activity* stories included all meetings, news conferences, speeches,
  and ceremonial activities that did not have a dominant policy
  theme. Also included were administrative decisions and appointments and nominations to federal agencies.

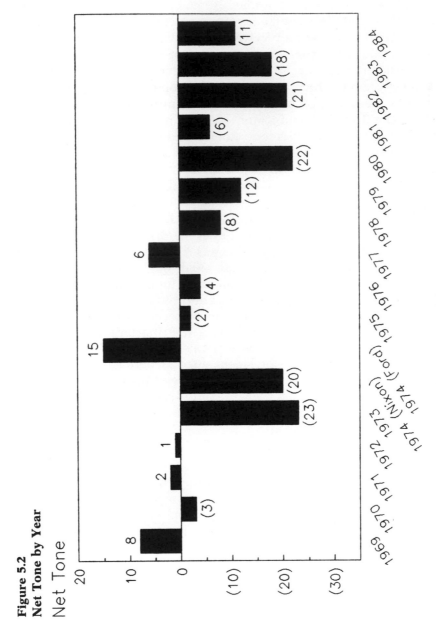

Figure 5.2
Net Tone by Year

50

Figure 5.3
Net Tone Scores by Six-Month Periods

Net Tone

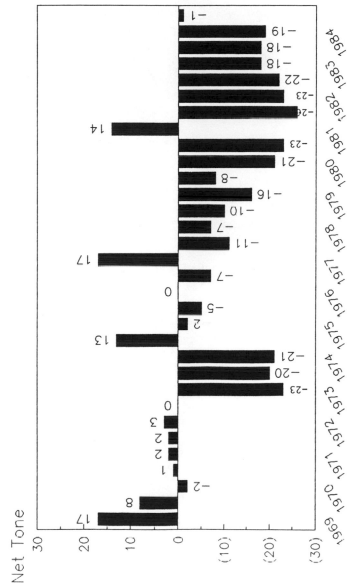

Figure 5.4
Content of Presidential News

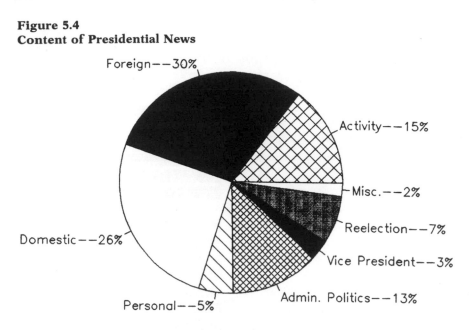

- *Foreign* policy stories included all dealings with other countries, trips abroad, and military affairs. Also included here were stories concerning the Secretary of State when it was clear that he was acting on the president's behalf.

- *Domestic* policy stories included all legislation and activity concerning domestic issues, including the budget, economy, and taxes.

- *Personal* stories included items about the president's character and personal traits, his health, emotional well-being, and integrity, as well as stories about the First Family.

- *Administration politics* stories included stories about the president's staff, political controversy in the White House, scandal, and relationships with Congress and the press, interest groups, and the bureaucracy. All Watergate stories were included here.

- *Vice president* stories included items about the vice president.

- *Reelection* stories included all stories concerning election activity by the president.

- *Miscellaneous* included the small number of stories that did not fit into the other categories. Stories that concerned the office of the U.S. presidency—what the framers intended, for example—were included in this category.

The Stable Categories

Little change was reported in the following categories: personal, administration politics, reelection, and vice president.

Five percent of the stories considered focused specifically on the president's personal life. Some 13 percent of the stories focused on administrative politics. (If Nixon's "Watergate" term is excluded, this percentage drops to 7.) Just 3 percent of the stories coded were about the vice president. Spiro Agnew attracted much attention during the first Nixon administration because of his attacks on student protestors and the media. He was also widely covered during the second Nixon administration when his criminal activities were reported by the press and he was forced to resign. Nelson Rockefeller was heavily covered (for a vice president) during the Ford administration; most of this coverage concerned whether Rockefeller was going to be dropped from Ford's 1976 reelection ticket. Untroubled but relatively active vice presidents such as Walter Mondale and George Bush, however, have received virtually no coverage on the evening news—less than 2 percent of the stories.

Activity stories dropped from 18 percent of the stories in the Nixon administration to 12 percent in the Reagan administration. This suggests that CBS may be less inclined to cover stories that focus solely on official presidential activities, like laying wreaths or taking part in a ceremony. Since such stories tended to be covered favorably, this decline could be one of the reasons there has been a drop in the percentage of positive stories and the overall tone of presidential news has become more negative (Table 5.3).

The "Prime-Time" Policy Advocate

Presidents appeared in the evening news primarily as policy advocates. This was the focus of more than half of the stories. Fifty-six percent of the coverage Nixon received during his first term was devoted to foreign and domestic policy. (Lower policy percentages were recorded in Nixon's second term because of Watergate, whereas the number of administration politics stories rose sharply.) Gerald Ford did not have the time or the electoral mandate to introduce a comprehensive legislative program to Congress—thus, the lower percentage (47) of policy-related stories in his administration. Sixty percent of the coverage of the Carter administration concerned domestic and foreign policy stories. The comparable figure for Reagan was 67. (See Table 5.3.)

Table 5.3
Content of Presidential News by Administration (percentages)

Subject	Nixon(1)	Nixon	Ford	Carter	Reagan
Activity	18	11	19	13	12
Foreign	29	19	28	31	35
Domestic	27	11	19	29	32
Personal	3	8	6	6	3
Amin. Pol	8	43	6	8	10
Vice Pres	6	5	5	1	1
Reelect.	5	1	15	10	6
Misc.	3	2	2	1	1

Why the increase in policy coverage? One reason is that break-throughs in technology (Chapter 3) have made foreign affairs coverage much easier. Where once anchormen listened to static-filled phone conversations from their overseas correspondents, crystal-clear video signals are now available via satellite from virtually anywhere on earth. Pictures from overseas locales provide enticing visuals, whether or not the president is making news.

Another possible explanation for the boost in policy stories is the in-creased emphasis CBS placed on policy evaluation during the early 1980s. Policy evaluation stories seek to assess the impact of the presi-dent's policies, particularly his domestic programs. But rather than focus on dry statistics that are often difficult to explain and compre-hend, producers at CBS were urged to incorporate "moments" into their pieces. A *moment* is a visually and emotionally absorbing scene in a news story that appeals to a viewer's heart rather than to his or her head. In his comprehensive study of CBS News, Peter Boyer (1988:139) explains the impact the "moments doctrine" had on the news coverage of Ronald Reagan's economic program:

> What the moments doctrine amounted to, of course, was a deftly de-
> signed cover for the infiltration of entertainment values into the news. It
> completely changed the way CBS reported the day's news because it com-
> pletely changed what news was. There were no moments to be found in a
> minute-fifteen report on unemployment told by a CBS News correspon-
> dent standing outside the Department of Labor in Washington, D.C.
> There was, however, a moment of the highest sort if the CBS News cam-

era studied the strained and expectant face of a young Pittsburgh mother as she stood (babe in arms) beside an employment line as her husband asked for a job. And if the CBS News camera was patient enough to remain focused until the husband was told there was no work, it was jackpot city.

The coding scheme was not designed to measure moments. But I did code the location from which stories were reported. If there has been an increase in policy assessment stories (including such moments as the one described above), then there should be an increase in stories set outside the nation's Capitol, in places like Pittsburgh, where the impact of the president's programs are felt.

"Setting" codes were assigned according to the following definitions:

- *Anchor* reports are stories read by the anchorman from his desk in the studio.
- *Washington* stories are reported by a correspondent from various locations inside the Beltway (primarily the White House but also Capitol Hill and the Federal Courthouse).
- *United States* stories are reported from outside the Beltway but within the United States.
- *Overseas* stories are set *overseas*.

I used the correspondent's sign-off line—"This is Leslie Stahl at the White House"—to determine the setting code (see Figure 5.5).

Table 5.4 shows that there has been a decrease in anchor reports and an increase in the number of stories reported from Washington and from outside the Capitol. The percentage of stories reported from outside the Capitol doubled—from 7 percent in the Nixon administration (first term) to 14 percent in the Reagan administration. This increase becomes more apparent when we look just at domestic policy stories. In a separate analysis I found that only 3 percent of the domestic policy stories in Richard Nixon's first term were set outside of Washington. During Ronald Reagan's first term, the figure was 19 percent.[10]

Tone

The increase in negative coverage also seems to be based broadly, covering a number of different dimensions of the presidency. Table 5.5 shows the signs of the net tone scores for each content category, for

Figure 5.5
Setting of Presidential News

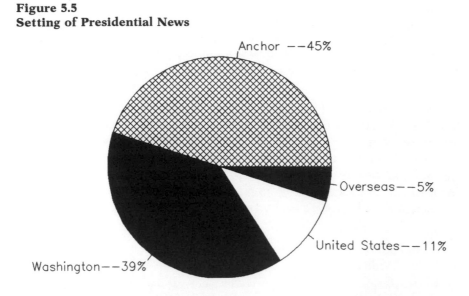

each administration. The first Nixon administration received net posi-tive coverage in four of the eight categories. None of the following administrations received net positive coverage in more than two cate-gories. Activity stories received net positive coverage for all presi-dents—even for Richard Nixon during his Watergate term. Domestic policy and administrative politics stories were negative for all presi-dents. The net tone of foreign policy stories moved from positive in the Nixon administration to neutral in the Ford and Carter administrations to negative in Reagan's. No clear pattern emerged in the remaining categories. If a category was coded negative during the first Nixon ad-ministration, in no case did it become positive in a subsequent admin-istration. Thus, the toughening of news coverage is not limited to one or two subject areas that are covered exclusively; instead, it seems to be occurring across a range of topics.

Cronkite and Rather

Another indication of the growing negativity of news coverage of the president is the tone of the reports presented by the anchors and com-mentators. The anchorman is the mainstay of the broadcast. He is both the manager and the star player of the team. As managing editor, he, along with the executive producer, decides the lineup of stories for each night's telecast. He is involved in important personnel and policy

Table 5.4
Setting of Presidential News by Administration

Setting	Nixon(1)	Nixon	Ford	Carter	Reagan
Studio	57	48	44	41	41
Washington	32	42	39	41	40
United States	7	7	13	13	14
Overseas	4	3	4	5	5

decisions. His values, beliefs, and behavior set the tone for the entire broadcast. When he is replaced, much of the direction and focus of the program shifts accordingly. Such was the case when on March 9, 1981, Dan Rather replaced Walter Cronkite as anchor. Was there a difference in the tone of their reports?[11]

Table 5.6 suggests that Dan Rather is more critical in his coverage of the presidency than his predecessor. Seventeen percent of Cronkite's reports were positive, 62 percent were neutral, and 21 percent were negative. Only 8 percent of Rather's reports were positive, 68 percent were neutral, and 24 percent were negative. The net tone score for Cronkite, who covered the Vietnam War and Watergate and the pardoning of Richard Nixon, was −4; Rather, who covered one of the twentieth century's most popular presidents, had a net tone score of −16.

Sevareid and Moyers

I also compared the tone of the commentaries provided by Eric Sevareid and Bill Moyers. Eric Sevareid provided commentary on a regular basis from fall 1963 until November 1977. Bill Moyers provided commentary intermittently from 1979 through 1986. I coded 185 commentaries for Sevareid but only 20 for Moyers (Table 5.6). Twenty-seven percent of Sevareid's commentaries were positive, 51 percent were neutral, and 22 percent were negative. His net tone was +5. Moyers's figures were: 25 percent positive, 25 percent neutral, and 50 percent negative. His net tone was −25. When I presented these results to him, Sevareid was not surprised: "I once told Bill that I was 70 percent teacher and 30 percent preacher; whereas he was 30 percent teacher and 70 percent preacher. And he agreed. My job was to report and explain, more than advocate. I felt I should tell the people what they ought to be thinking about, the historical context in which things were occurring. Bill had a different view."[12]

Table 5.5
Net Tone by Administration, by Content

	Nixon(1)	Nixon(2)	Ford	Carter	Reagan
Activity	+	+	+	+	+
Foreign	+	+	0	0	-
Domestic	-	-	-	-	-
Personal	+	-	+	-	+
Admin. Pol	-	-	-	-	-
Vice Pres.	0	-	0	+	-
Reelect.	+	0	-	-	0
Misc	-	-	0	-	-

+ Positive Net Tone
- Negative Net Tone
0 Neutral--Balance of Positive and Negative Stories

The differences in the tone of the anchor reports and commentators reflect, in part, changes in media attitudes toward the presidency. Cronkite and Sevareid are part of the "old breed" of former print reporters who covered World War II for CBS Radio. They were also part of a generation of Americans who celebrated the growth of presidential power. Rather and Moyers are part of a second generation of journalists at CBS who came of age professionally during the 1960s and 1970s— for Moyers, press secretary for Lyndon Johnson, during the reign of the imperial presidency and, for Rather, during an age when the news division faced increased pressure to cut costs and increase revenues. By leaning harder on the president, they were able to satisfy their organization's need for improved ratings while, as journalists, performing their watchdog role.

CONCLUSION

This chapter has shown empirical support for the contention that CBS News covers the president extensively and in a negative fashion. Approximately 20 percent of a typical evening news program focuses on the president. While the bulk of the coverage is neutral, the majority of directional (positive or negative) coverage is negative. It has also

Table 5.6
Anchors and Commentators

	Positive	Neutral	Negative	Net Tone
Cronkite	17	63	21	-4
Rather	8	68	24	-16
Sevareid	27	51	22	5
Moyers	25	25	50	-25

been shown, in a variety of ways, that television news coverage is getting tougher on the president:

1. Each full-term president received more unfavorable coverage than his predecessor.
2. Presidential honeymoons with the press are ending more abruptly and decisively.
3. No president since Richard Nixon (first term) has received a net positive portrayal after his first six months in office.
4. The increase in negative coverage is broadly based, affecting several dimensions of the presidency.
5. Anchors and commentators, the focal points of the broadcast, are leaning harder on the White House.

Extensive negative coverage is the bedrock of the six o'clock presidency thesis. Now the question arises, How and why does news coverage of the president vary during the course of a president's term? It is to this question that we now turn.

NOTES

1. Other variables coded: case, deck, year, month, day, date, reporter, type (news story or editorial), setting, and the source and object of criticisms made of the president and his policies.
2. There are 5,844 days between January 1, 1969, and January 20, 1985; there are 52 weekends in a year, for a total of 104 days: $5,844 - (104 \times 16) = 4,180$.
3. Grossman and Kumar (1981), for example, examined 452 stories over a 23-year period (1954–77).
4. The precise figure is 2.16 ($1,800/832 = 2.16$).
5. The sample broke down like this: Mondays, 18.5 percent; Tuesdays, 21

percent; Wednesdays, 20.4 percent; Thursdays, 20.4 percent; and Fridays, 19.3 percent.

6.   The estimation of 12 to 15 stories per program was suggested by Jack Smith, CBS News Washington bureau chief.

7.   Fifteen randomly selected program transcripts were used to generate the mean number of lines per program.

8.   Presidential stories are also given a prominent position in the broadcast. CBS led its broadcast with a White House story in 14 percent of the cases examined. A presidential report appeared in rank 2 through 5 in 35 percent of the cases. The remaining 51 percent appeared in ranks 6 through 10.

9.   A variety of approaches were used to measure story tone. Initially I calculated the net percentage of positive, neutral, and negative transcript lines. This was done to compensate for the fact that stories delivered by the anchorman tend to be shorter than correspondent stories. Anchors also present a greater proportion of neutral stories (e.g., the routine coverage of presidential appointments and announcements). I also calculated the ratios of positive and negative stories, to compensate for variations in cases across the years. Regardless of the measure, the same basic patterns of coverage emerged. The measure "net tone" was used because it is the simplest, the most straightforward, and the easiest to explain.

10.   To my surprise, the percentage of foreign policy stories reported from overseas remained stable. The percentage of foreign policy stories reported by the anchor has declined. But we did not find the increase in reports set overseas that we anticipated. While the percentage of stories that focus on the president's foreign policies has increased, and while overseas footage has become more accessible, the bulk of the foreign policy stories coded is still set in Washington.

11.   Some may question the "fairness" of comparing the two anchors, since we have reports from 12 years for Cronkite and only 4 for Rather (as anchor). Moreover, Cronkite served as anchor for three administrations (during the Nixon, Ford, and Carter administrations and two months of the Reagan administration), whereas Rather served as anchor during only one administration (Reagan). Nevertheless the number of reports is sizable: 1,461 for Cronkite; 452 for Rather.

12.   Interview with Eric Sevareid, September 19, 1989. Richard Salant, former CBS News president, concurs with this view: "We put Eric Sevareid on virtually every night to explain things to the American people that we couldn't show them in pictures, such as the structure of the Office, and the constraints which inhibit the exercise of presidential power." Sevareid said that many producers objected to his commentaries, feeling that they could replace him with something "hotter." Moyers, incidentally, is an ordained Baptist minister.

6

The Four Seasons of Presidential News

As the information business has become highly profitable, presidents, their families, their associates, their friends—even their pets—have turned into the raw material that fuels a major industry . . . . The issue is not whether reporters like the president or agree with him . . . . It is a matter of whether or not a president is "good copy."

Stephen Hess[1]

Having marshaled evidence suggesting the scope and negative bias of White House news, this chapter suggests how the content and tone of television news vary during the course of a presidential term.

Before we begin, the reader should know that the argument presented here is more suggestive and less definitive than the arguments presented in the previous chapters. During the coding of the data, I noted what I believe to be interesting and important thematic patterns. By this time, however, it was not possible to alter the coding procedures to allow for a more rigorous exploration of the data. Nevertheless, I believe these patterns are important, and I want to present them to you. I also want to alert future researchers that this is a promising area for exploration. With this caveat in mind, let us proceed.

PUBLIC OPINION AND THE PRESIDENCY

Media researchers disagree about the extent to which the image of the presidency that appears in the evening news actually influences citizen attitudes toward the president. Some feel TV news has only a minimal impact on citizen attitudes (Patterson and McClure, 1976; Robinson and Levy, 1986). Others maintain that public opinion, not the media, determines the long-term pattern of media coverage of the president (Buchanan, 1987). Experimental research suggests that the evening news does influence how people think about political candidates and national problems (Iyengar, Peters, and Kinder, 1982).

This study found that the amount of positive coverage the president receives correlates with his level of public support. Figure 6.1 shows the correlation between Gallup support scores and the percentage of positive news stories for six-month periods (r = .64, R^2 = .41) from 1969 to 1984.[2] The results, though not conclusive, do suggest that the image of the president that appears in nightly news programs—as campaign managers and White House aides readily attest—is an important determinant of how people think about the president. The question remains, How do people process presidential news?

FOCUS GROUP RESEARCH

A focus group discussion a colleague and I conducted in 1981 shed some light on this question (Smoller and Fitzgerald, 1981). A *focus group* is simply a group discussion led by a moderator along predetermined topical lines. Focus groups are ideally suited to exploratory research because of their sensitivity, flexibility, and low cost. The importance of focus groups lies in the existence of a free-flowing dialogue that provides the researcher insight into political reasoning that cannot be gained through more structured techniques. Our discussion, which was held in Bloomington, Indiana, during April 1981 centered primarily on the Carter and Reagan presidencies.

THE USE OF STEREOTYPES

During the course of the group discussion and subsequent interviews, we were struck by the role that media-based stereotypes play in presidential evaluation. As one participant commented:

> I think it is amazing how much style counts. The difference between walking into a hospital after getting shot and beating off a killer rabbit

Figure 6.1
Gallup Support Scores and Net Tone

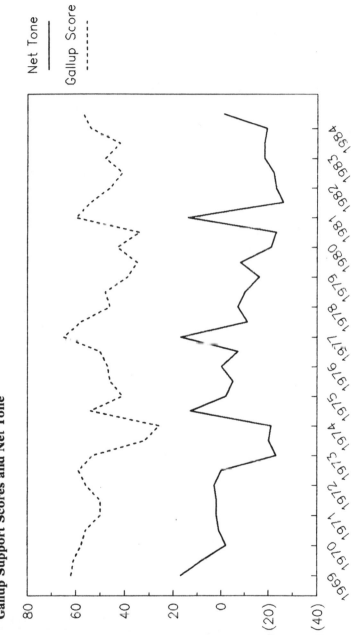

with an oar somehow seems to typify the difference between the two presidents for me.

By paying attention, however vicariously, to the news (as well as the other agents of socialization such as one's parents, schools, and friends), citizens come to form an impression of the president. This impression cannot be described as comprehensive, well organized, or causal. Although rather vague in detail and impressionistic, this scheme is used to simplify and explain a whole variety of presidential behavior, past and present. For instance, Carter's "poor" handling of the Soviet's invasion of Afghanistan implied to many that he was indecisive and unsuccessful in other areas as well, despite a respectable legislative record that included, for example, a comprehensive energy program, the long-needed reform of the Civil Service Program, and the passage of the Panama Canal treaties. As the same participant commented:

> He lacked the ability to make me believe that he was in control, and I lost confidence in him. He seemed indecisive in foreign policy. He was the master of the overstatement. The invasion of Afghanistan became the biggest threat to world peace since World War II. There have been a lot of things that have happened that were more important than the invasion of Afghanistan. On the domestic front, for example, Carter was unable to get through some very important legislation—energy, for instance, which was the pressing issue during his administration.

Reagan's response to the attempt on his life and his early string of domestic legislative successes implied to some that he was doing equally well in foreign policy. But at the time the group was conducted—April 1981—the president had yet to amass an impressive record in foreign policy.

Language plays a crucial role in the attitude formation process by providing a framework for structuring political evaluations. Citizens seem to "pick up" certain words or phrases that have received prominence in the media. Once people have taken the suggestion that a political actor is "stupid and clumsy" or a "hatch man" or a "great communicator," all behavior may be seen in this light.

THE THEMATIC NATURE OF TELEVISION NEWS

Because people use stereotypes to simplify complex political phenomena, this is how television communicates its message. Scholars have repeatedly noted the use of "themes" as one of the distinguishing characteristics of television news (Altheide, 1976; Braestrup, 1978; Robinson and Sheehan, 1983; Nimmo and Combs, 1985).

The networks organize their reports around agreed-upon themes to make them accessible and entertaining to as wide an audience as possible. In order not to confuse viewers, editors, for example, routinely discard dialogue and videotape that do not support the prevailing theme of a news report: A story about the White House losing a major fight on Capitol Hill would not include videotape of the president smiling. Likewise, care is taken to make sure that news reports in a particular segment of the program (usually between commercials) dovetail together (Epstein, 1973a).

Themes also tie continuing news stories together. By structuring reports around underlying themes, correspondents are able to update big stories without having to repeat everything that has been previously reported. Correspondents remind viewers of the relevant theme before proceeding with new information (Chancellor and Mears, 1983:48). For example, here is a lead-in by anchor Roger Mudd to a story by Lee Thornton about a trip President Carter took down the Mississippi River to promote his energy policies (CBS News transcript, August 15, 1979). The underlying theme is that this is a troubled presidency, and the president's press problems are one more example of his ineffectiveness in office:

> *Roger Mudd*: As if President Carter is not having enough trouble with his Cabinet, his staff, the economy and the price of gasoline, he is now being accused of managing the news. The charge comes from the news organizations which had thought that a presidential trip on a Mississippi stern-wheeler would be a photographer's dream. Lee Thornton reports.

Themes are also reinforced by news producers who routinely reject or fail to commission material that is inconsistent with or appears to contradict the broader theme of a continuing story. For example, shortly after he was chosen as the 1972 Democratic vice presidential nominee, it was revealed that Thomas Eagleton had been hospitalized on several occasions for emotional stress and had received electric-shock treatments. These revelations raised genuine questions about whether or not Eagleton was fit for the job. Media analyst David Altheide (1976), however, argues persuasively that the dominant theme—When was Eagleton going to be dropped from the ticket?—discouraged such inquiries. Likewise, the networks organized their coverage of the hostage crisis in Iran during the Carter administration around the theme: When would the hostages be released? Stories that did not fit that theme (e.g., stories about the history of U.S. involvement in Iran or the abuses of power that had been committed by the shah or the nature of the Islamic revolution) received little attention (Altheide, 1981).

THE FOUR SEASONS OF PRESIDENTIAL NEWS

The use of thematic stereotypes reduces the overwhelming complexity of the presidency to a simple message that meets the needs of the commercial networks and, when favorable to the incumbent, the desires of his administration. The message is limited at the source (1) by the White House's monopoly of information about the president; (2) by correspondents who must keep their reports short, uncomplicated, and entertaining; and (3) by producers who edit news stories to be internally consistent and who systematically reject stories that do not fit the prevailing story line.

These factors combine to produce an internally consistent, simple, and uniform story line about the president—a story line that takes the form of a continuing evaluation of the president's performance in office. Simply, this is a theme that the networks have the resources and inclination to address on a continuing basis. The need for the news to be simple produces a consistent story line about the president, whereas the need for the news to be novel produces variations in this story line over time.

Having established the need for a consistent presidential story line, in this section we will show (1) how the inordinate amount of attention paid the president moves the tone of presidential news from positive to negative and (2) how the need for consistency causes the increasingly negative tone to color divergent aspects of presidential news.

Each season is distinguished by the content and tone of news coverage. Coverage proceeds from a uniformly positive appraisal to a uniformly negative appraisal because of the *perceived inadequacies* of the president's policies. A network's need to present a consistent image of the president contributes to a homogenous portrayal of seemingly unrelated dimensions of the presidency: presidential activities, domestic policies, and the president's personal life.

Once the story line is established (for example, "The president has tremendous promise" or "He is incompetent and is fighting for his political life"), this view colors divergent aspects of White House coverage. This results in dissimilar or only tangentially related White House activities becoming tainted for no logical reason and the reporting of divergent activities so as to reinforce a uniform portrayal of the president's performance in office. This reporting produces a swing in the tone of presidential news coverage from the president as an "across-the-board success" to the president as a "total failure." Here is how CBS White House correspondent Leslie Stahl talks about a report she put together about Ronald Reagan:

> I called the bureau and said, "You know, I've been thinking—Reagan has been losing everywhere. He is losing on the nuclear freeze initiative. He is losing the battle of the budget. He is losing on defense. He is losing on his Central America policy, and he is losing on arms control. Everything has changed around for him. I think I would like to do a piece on where he is now—why he's losing and what is happening."

This transformation takes place through four seasons of news coverage. During the first stage, presidents, their staffs, and their families are profiled. In the second stage, news coverage shifts to the president's domestic legislative agenda being introduced in Congress. In the third stage, this program is evaluated prematurely, primarily by Washington-based elites (congressional leaders, interest group heads, movers and shakers in the media and the bureaucracy). In the fourth and final stage, presidents are reevaluated. In short, the president is profiled, and then his policies are examined; these policies are evaluated, and then the president is reevaluated.

Personal Profile

The network's commitment to extensive coverage of a new president begins during the electoral season. Network news profoundly influences modern presidential campaigns. Almost all activities are geared to news coverage. Such coverage can legitimize a candidate as a serious contender—sometimes before that judgment is borne out in public opinion polls or primary victories.

As overseer of U.S. politics, one of the network's chief functions is to reveal new candidates to the public. This process takes place to some extent during the campaign. Coverage of the "horse race," however, crowds out more extensive profiling of the candidates. But once the race is concluded in November, network news, along with the other media, profiles the new president, his family, and staff. The focus is on the president and those close to him—family, friends, and chief aides. News coverage is usually very favorable; the president is all potential at this point.

Never again will coverage be as favorable.

The presidential family is the centerpiece of many news stories during the personality profile stage. The eccentric mother and boisterous brother are novel and amusing. White House aides will be portrayed as competent. They have "hit the ground running." The organizational skills that masterminded the president's nomination and election will pay off well in the Oval Office. The president is portrayed as uniquely qualified for the job. Thus, during the personal profile stage, coverage of most aspects of the presidency is positive in tone. Here is an example of a personal profile story from the first Nixon administration.

> *Cronkite*: Good evening. In his first day on the job, President Nixon has made it clear that his will be an early bird administration. He showed up for work ahead of his staff today, probably the last time they'll let that happen, and for tomorrow he has scheduled a White House ceremony for eight o'clock in the morning. Dan Rather reports.

> *Rather*: At 7:30 A.M. the President was working in his office, although he had gone to bed after the Inaugural Balls less than six hours earlier. He told reporters he does not intend to do all of his work in the traditional Oval Office at the White House's West Wing, said he intends to have his real work office across the street in the Executive Office Building. He believes he will be disturbed less often with an office out of the White House.
>
> The new White House staff has moving boxes stacked everywhere, is having a difficult time finding where various other offices are located, and finds itself undermanned because all of the new personnel hiring has not been completed. But ready or not, the Nixons and their staffs hosted 1300 of the party faithful at the East Room rally today. The President heaped praise on his campaign workers, on his family and on Vice President Spiro Agnew. He promised to start early and work late most days, and repeated that warning later at a swearing in ceremony for his new staff. Mr. Nixon emphasized that White House life under him, as under Lyndon Johnson, would be harried.

Here is another personal profile story that was aired August 13, 1974, during the Ford administration:

> *Mudd*: Mrs. Gerald Ford took a close look today at the House she will move into next week, and then she went home to start packing. Susan Peterson reports.

> *Peterson*: It is customary for the departing First Lady to conduct a White House tour for the incoming family. But the Nixon's sudden departure made it impossible. Instead, the White House Chief Usher guided Mrs. Ford and her daughter, Susan, through the private quarters where they'll begin living next Monday. Later, Mrs. Ford told reporters she didn't plan to make any major change in decor.

And from the Carter administration, which aired on January 27, 1977:

> *Cronkite*: Although winter has seized the capital, there's a warm drawl of you-all in the Washington air. The Georgians have arrived. And Roger Mudd tells us about it.
>
> *Mudd*: Roosevelt brought the New York Brain Trust. Johnson surrounded himself with Texans. Nixon imported the California Mafia. Today, the White House is crammed with Georgians, and Washington has been seized by Georgia mania.

Coverage of the president focuses on personality issues because his president legislative agenda is not yet available. The network's reliance on the presidency for news, and the presumed high audience interest in the new administration, means that the president will be extensively profiled, especially since such stories involve little or no research, are easily explained, and are entertaining. The White House is, not surprisingly, very cooperative during the personal profile stage.

The duration of the personal profile stage is a function of several phenomena. Well-known public figures will tend to have shorter profile periods than fresh faces. Also, presidential aides skilled in public relations, or the intervention of events (such as an assassination attempt), may serve to prolong the profiling stage. Presidents who make a particularly good first impression with members of Congress, the press, and the mass public will also have more extensive profiles. At some point, however, the profiling stage comes to a close, as CBS White House correspondent Leslie Stahl notes:

> Revealing the president to the public is part of the job. But once you have revealed him, you don't want to do it 50,000 times. I always hear from my producers, "We've done that story; we've done that story." You hear that a lot from people who put broadcasts on.

Legislative Proposal

The personal profile stage is closely followed by the legislative proposal stage. Network news attention shifts to the president's legislative agenda now being introduced in Congress, focusing on policy substance and on the politics of persuasion. The frequency of stories that profile the president and his family declines, whereas the number of stories about the president's proposed programs increases. The tone of stories concerning the president becomes increasingly negative as press coverage focuses on the president's attempt to push his program through the Congress. Here are Walter Cronkite and correspondent Phil Jones, CBS News, reporting on the president's budget proposals as they wind their way through the Senate. These stories aired on January 27, 1977 and March 27, 1981.

> *Cronkite*: Good evening. The Carter Administration said today the $50 a person tax rebate checks could be in mailboxes within three months. But that depends on quick Congressional approval of the President's economic stimulation plan. And key Carter economic advisors warned Congress that too much tinkering with the plan could ruin it. George Herman reports. . . .
>
> *Rather:* Here in Washington Senate debate of the Reagan budget-cut package turned acrimonious today along party lines. Phil Jones listened to it.
>
> *Jones:* Senate Republicans couldn't keep from gloating today. Quipped one, "The sun is really shining on the Capital. We are just kicking the you-know-what out of the Democrats." And inside, Democrats were indeed outnumbered and frustrated. Republicans knew that Democrats planned to push for restoration of at least $450-million in the Reagan-requested $1.6-billion cut in the school lunch program. So Republican Helms beat them to the punch.

The following story aired on April 14, 1969, about 2.5 months into Richard Nixon's first term. It illustrates the pressure the White House is under to get their legislative agenda to the Congress.

> *Reasoner*: Good evening. President Nixon sent to Congress today the broad outlines of his domestic legislative program. In what amounted to his own State of the Union message, the President set forth the areas and the general direction in which he wants to work, but left the details for later. Dan Rather reports.
>
> *Rather*: No President since William Howard Taft has asked Congress for so little, and Mr. Nixon was beginning to come under heavy criticism *for the slow pace of his administration in dealing with domestic problems* [emphasis added]. Over the weekend, pressure from congressional Republicans for the President to say, to do, something apparently reached such heights that Mr. Nixon felt he had to. He rushed out a five-page statement which is, in effect, a plea for more time. The President explained that the top priority in his administration thus far has gone to peace and battling inflation. Also, he said he needed time for a systematic review of all domestic policies. At any rate, the President says he is now ready with his recommendation, and they include these: increased Social Security benefits, new efforts to battle organized crime, tax incentives for private enterprise involved in social reform, more equal employment opportunity laws,

reorganization of the Post Office Department, a sharing of federal tax revenues with cities and states, new programs for airports and mass transit, labor and manpower programs, with special emphasis on safety, and federal tax reform.

All of these recommendations, Mr. Nixon promises, now are ready to flow to Congress, *in time, he hopes, to mute the building criticism that his was becoming a do-nothing administration on domestic welfare* [emphasis added].

Policy (Premature) Evaluation

After the initial policies have been considered, network news attention soon shifts to a preliminary evaluation of their effectiveness: who will they benefit and hurt? Are they safe? Are they fair? What do the other political actors think of them? Are they consistent? Do they contradict the president's campaign promises? And most of all, (do they) will they work?

Here is the rub: Because the evaluation stage takes place before the effects of the president's program can be felt, and because most contemporary political problems are long term in nature and require sacrifice, it is typical for a president's policies to be found misguided and inadequate, especially since this evaluation is often based on interviews with affected interest groups and other political elites headquartered in Washington, who tend to evaluate the president more harshly and more prematurely than the rest of the nation.

The networks have devised a variety of measures of presidential popularity and the success of the president's policies. They report the results of polling organizations such as Gallup. They also, in collaboration with major news organizations (e.g., *New York Times* and the *Washington Post*), commission their own polls. They also report the economic statistics in monthly terms and report the president's reaction. The tone of news stories concerning the president's domestic policies therefore becomes increasingly negative.

During the policy evaluation stage, network news coverage also focuses on administration politics, scandal, and conflict among the president's advisers. Hints of scandal involving administrative aides, or inappropriate appointments that may have been known earlier but were put aside due to the rush of news stories from the Capitol, can now be pursued.

Administration politics is especially amenable to network coverage because such stories generally require few resources, take place in Washington, can be obtained through interviews, involve conflict and drama, and have easily identifiable combatants. White House officials, in order to put off or limit political damage, sometimes inadvertently cooperate with the network by withholding information. Thus, the truth is unraveled in conveniently sized and spaced developments (that can be covered in less than two minutes) over an extended period of time. Administration politics stories fit into the overall evaluative theme. During the policy evaluation stage, then, these hints of inequity, ineptness, and scandal are likely to do considerable damage to a president's support among the public.

The need for the networks to give a homogenous portrayal of the president, and the central importance of trust and competence to any evaluation, causes this negative evaluation to influence the reporting of many other aspects of presidential news. So news coverage of the president's personal life and his activities becomes increasingly negative. The presidential family and friends can now become a political liability, and the shortcomings of the president and his aides are now highlighted.

Here is a policy evaluation story from the Reagan administration. It aired October 14, 1982.

> *Rather*: Three footnotes today to President Reagan's campaign speech last night about the economy. A Labor Department report released today says 695,000 Americans filed claims for unemployment benefits the week ending October 2nd. That's the second highest level this year.
>
> (Voice over) And among those filing claims recently was this man, ballet dancer Ronald Prescott Reagan for the Joffrey Company. He is President Reagan's son. In fact, as his father prepared for his speech last night, young Ron was giving a benefit performance—not dancing: standing and filing for benefits in a New York City unemployment line. Today he said he was one of forty Joffrey Company dancers on temporary layoff.
>
> *Reagan*: Laid off until October 25th, and as far as I know everybody's collecting unemployment. I am too; I'm no different.
>
> *Question*: The White House says that—that your father offered to support you, but that you turned him down and wanted to be independent.
>
> *Reagan*: I guess they knew better than I did that this sort of nonsense was going to happen, so they offered to give me a way out, and I said no, that's not necessary.

Television coverage of policy inadequacy, political infighting, scandal, as well as the personal shortcomings of the president necessarily follows the initial policy agenda because after the initial presidential proposals have been made, there is little else of substance to cover about the incumbent. However, the perceived need of having to have news about the president at six o'clock every evening, in conjunction with the constraints that influence that coverage, necessarily leads to finding fault with the administration. Given the initial positive evaluations, there is simply nowhere else to go.

It is important to stress that it is the *perceived* failure of the president's domestic policies to rapidly solve problems that causes negative coverage of other aspects of the president—not the other way around. Initial negative reports about the president's family or staff are simply not central enough to the role of the presidency to undercut the perception of the president as a competent leader during the personal profile and legislative proposal stages. It is only when the network's agenda is cleared that stories concerning the president's effectiveness and moral conduct can be vigorously pursued, with the result being a change in the reporting theme.

Presidential Reassessment

The cumulative effect of negative presidential news coverage brings on the fourth and final stage of the dynamic wherein the original positive evaluation of the president is reassessed. News reports questioning the president's competence become more frequent. He is clumsy and socially awkward; he makes verbal mistakes; his intelligence or moral qualities are less than acceptable. These reports create the impression of incompetence, ineptness, and failure on behalf of the president. Thereafter, the story line becomes the decline of the administration and the inability of the president to stop it.

This story aired August 7, 1979:

> *Mudd*: It's not often in Washington, that a departing Cabinet officer talks about the President the way Griffin Bell has been talking about Mr. Carter. Yesterday, at a farewell breakfast with reporters, Bell said firmly but gently that his old friend, Mr. Carter, was trying "to act like he wasn't President," that he wasted too much time working on minor problems. "The American people," said Bell, "want the President to act like a President. . . ."

> *Rather*: With campaign '82 now in the stretch run, Bill Plante reports today's White House guest list really ran the gamut, from a marathon race winner, who embarrassed Mr. Reagan a little, to the latest winner of the Nobel prize for economics, who embarrassed the White House a lot.

During this stage, high-level aides and the president himself will spend an inordinate amount of time on image-making and image-enhancing activities, with the result being less time spent on substantive issues.

In the beginning of a president's term, the White House attempts to use the media to marshal support for its legislative program. Later, however, these efforts are much more defensive in nature and are aimed primarily at keeping the level of negative news coverage to a minimum.

Most important, the erosion of support that will accompany the presidential reevaluation stage will make it more difficult for the president to govern—to get his programs through the Congress, to bargain effectively with foreign and domestic leaders, and to mediate conflicts among conflicting social, economic, and political interests. Because the networks have accelerated the evaluation process, new administrations have only a few short months to devise and implement their legislative agenda. This has led presidents and their staffs to grasp at often ill-conceived but broad-based policies (e.g., "supply-side economics"). An all-out effort is then exerted to drive these policies through the Congress. Such efforts invariably antagonize members of Congress, who believe that the legislature's role in the policy process has been preempted and who become bent on retaliation.

THE WHITE HOUSE RESPONSE

In an effort to recapture lost support, however, presidents often abuse their office, engage in covert activities, disregard the rights and liberties of individuals, and trample on the roles of other constitutional actors, most notably the Congress. During the 1960s, 1970s, and 1980s the presidency has been at the center of national scandal and national disgrace. Many of the abuses that originated here, however, can be attributed partly to a belief by presidents and their staffs that they could not maintain enough support to achieve their goals through legal channels.

It is the psychological effect brought on by lost public support, however, that is of greatest concern. The erosion of public support arguably places additional psychological pressures on the president (Buchanan, 1978). Presidents become increasingly frustrated because they are unable to get the "real" story of their administration to the American people. Because presidents may come to believe that their administration, their family, as well as themselves have been falsely and unfairly portrayed on the evening news, the internal moral barriers that may have prevented them from being less than truthful with the media (and therefore with the public) become lowered. The temptation to justify deceptive and illegal activities and outright lies is increased.

All these factors invariably increase the frustration the president experiences. In response to this stress, and in an often futile effort to secure their place in history, presidents have initiated unwise policies that have not been successful (e.g., Carter's ordering of the hostage rescue mission, which ultimately failed, and Reagan's involvement in the Iran-Contra initiative). When they do so, especially in the nuclear age, they jeopardize the security of the nation.

During the presidential reevaluation stage, relations between the press secretary and the press become increasingly strained. The White House institutes a campaign to stop leaks to the press. The president makes fewer appearances, and tighter restrictions are placed on television coverage of him. Presidents often turn to other media, particularly to radio or to "controlled" television (speeches, e.g.) to reach the public. Public relations efforts are increased, as greater efforts by the staff are made to counter the negative image of the president portrayed on the evening news. Some presidents grasp at new domestic initiatives, whereas others will do things that focus attention on themselves and their families (e.g., domestic trips and vacations) in a vain attempt to get more favorable coverage. Some presidents will simply isolate themselves.

More often, however, presidents attempt to counter the increasingly unfavorable portrayal by emphasizing those aspects of the presidency—foreign policy, for example—that are least amenable to the routines that produce negative coverage. Knowing television's weakness for good pictures, the White House will place the president in the most visually compelling situations possible. Scenes of Richard Nixon at the Great Wall of China, Jimmy Carter embracing Sadat and Begin, or Ronald Reagan riding horseback with the queen of England are so visually compelling that they will be the themes around which news stories will be based, regardless of the substantive impact of the activity involved. Presidents will also engage in activities that emphasize the symbolic trappings of the office. Critical coverage of such activities would put the networks in the awkward position of criticizing the office of the presidency.

In this chapter, we have seen how, over time, the network news personalizes (personal profile), exaggerates (legislative agenda), accelerates (policy evaluation), and frustrates (presidential reevaluation) the presidency.

Such coverage is characteristic of television news from the White House on a daily basis as well. Because television organizes its coverage of U.S. politics around the presidency, the networks foster the impression that the president is responsible for virtually all governmental

Figure 6.2
Outline of Argument

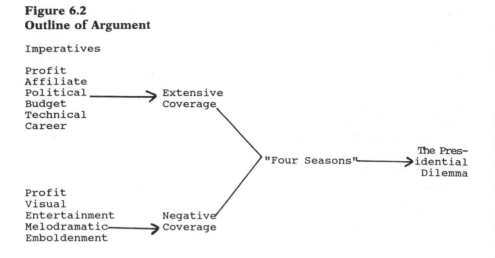

activities. The fact that the White House lawn has become the focal point of U.S. politics has reinforced this impression (Cutler, 1984). Citizens are apt to look solely to the presidency (as opposed to the Congress, the bureaucracy, or local or state government) for solutions to the nation's problems. One artificial heart patient, William Schroeder, even asked President Reagan to wrench a check from the Social Security Administration for him. (The ploy worked.)

Extensive coverage also exaggerates the power of the presidency. By lavishing attention on the White House, television has fostered the impression of a nearly indomitable chief executive. At the same time, television minimizes the power of less telegenic political actors, such as the Congress, special-interest groups, lobbyists, and especially the bureaucracy. Citizens are thereby encouraged to develop unrealistic performance expectations and to underestimate the web of constraint in which presidential action occurs.

Television news has also speeded up the process of presidential evaluation. Because they face a fixed term of office, presidents have always been pressured to devise, enact, and implement their programs as quickly as possible. Television, however, has cut down the time a new administration has to generate favorable results. Entertainers often complain that the medium has a voracious appetite for material. Celebrities are careful to avoid overexposure and thereby reduce the pressure to develop new material. Similarly, television has a voracious appetite for presidential action and accomplishment. Television's need for the news to be novel often means that presidents have to prove themselves to the American people on a daily basis. "What have you done for us lately?" (or "What have you done wrong lately?") is the underlying question correspondents pose to the White House each night. Each of these factors increases the frustration inherent in the job.

The next two chapters consider how the Carter and Reagan administrations have attempted to cope with the six o'clock presidency (see Figure 6.2). As we shall see, although administrations differ in their response to the six o'clock presidency, none has been able to completely transcend its consequences.

NOTES

1. Hess (1978:A11).
2. The "Net Tone" score did not produce as strong a correlation with the Gallup index.

7

The Carter Response

One of the great lessons I have learned from Watergate is to have a maximum amount of openness. I know I'll be very cautious as President to avoid any semblance of dishonesty or concealing information that the public has a right to know.

Jimmy Carter[1]

Most reporters don't have a direct professional interest in breaking the president. But because they feel they have to keep themselves on . . . the air, there is a bias—subconscious for the most part—against any institution that is covered on a full time basis. The result is the same. In fact, the result may even be worse for it being not a matter of malice or intent, but the way the process works.

Jody Powell,
Press Secretary to President Jimmy Carter[2]

THE PRESIDENTIAL DILEMMA

How have incumbents coped with the six o'clock presidency? Presidents face a dilemma when dealing with the press: their desire to be effective versus their presumed desire to preserve democratic values. Buchanan (1987:119) describes this dilemma:

> On the one hand, any president's pragmatic interest is in securing posi-
> tive, friendly media coverage. Favorable treatment is usually sought by
> managing the flow of news through the White House press office, con-
> trolling potentially damaging news leaks, cultivating individual reporters
> and editors in hopes of getting the president's point of view across and
> occasionally, seeking public sympathy through complaining of unfair,
> distorted or simplistic coverage.... On the other hand, most practicing
> political professionals, as well as journalists, acknowledge and believe in
> the First Amendment. They hold it as an article of democratic morality
> and professional ethics that presidents are obligated to disclose any infor-
> mation not demonstrably damaging to the national interest. The public's
> right to know is protected by a free press functioning as a democratic
> watchdog. A natural conflict arises: Full disclosure can be politically
> damaging, but complete or self-serving disclosure threatens to under-
> mine democratic accountability. Few modern presidents have succeeded
> in reconciling these inconsistent imperatives.

In dealing with the press, then, presidents must choose between two
undesirable postures. The first alternative—the "open" presidency—
emphasizes accessibility and accountability. The president holds news
conferences often, keeps his press secretary thoroughly informed, and
makes himself available to reporters on a regular basis. Efforts to manage the news are kept to a minimum. However, because the president
forgoes the opportunity to shape his televised image, he is particularly
vulnerable to the adverse consequences of extensive negative coverage. Such presidents are high on a democratic morality scale but tend
to be less effective because they forgo the opportunity to manage news
coverage of their administrations.

Press access is severely curtailed in the "closed" presidency. The
president holds press conferences infrequently, seldom takes questions
from reporters, and rarely reveals his thoughts or intentions to the
press. The press secretary is not privy to high-level policy decisions.
News management efforts are a key feature of the president's governing strategy.

With only a favorable portrayal upon which to base an appraisal, the
president is more likely to remain popular. Public support will en-
hance his effectiveness. His legislative proposals will be favorably received by Congress. His clout with foreign and domestic elites, and his
ability to influence key members of the bureaucracy in charge of implementing his agenda, will increase. The likelihood of his being reelected will also increase. However, because the president is not
subject to reporters' criticisms and questions on a regular basis, he is
more likely to become isolated. Poor decisions and policy mistakes

Figure 7.1
The Presidential Dilemma

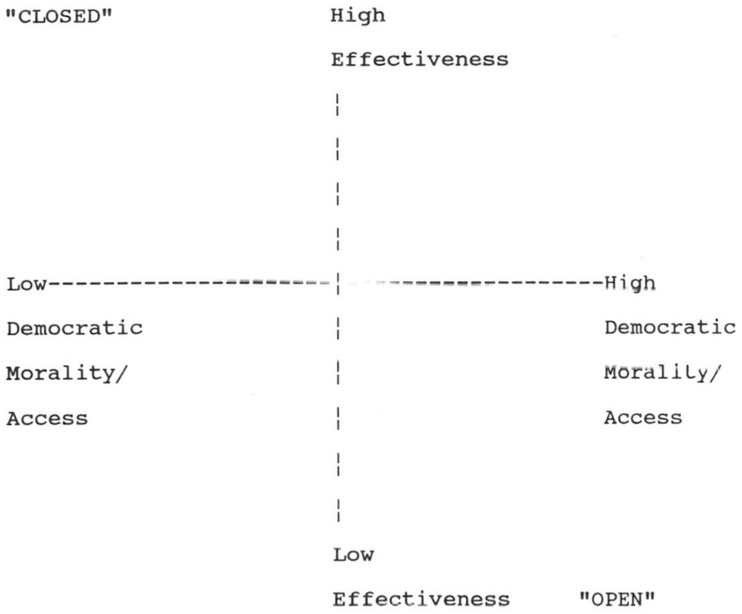

```
    "CLOSED"                    High

                            Effectiveness

                                |

                                |

                                |

                                |

    Low---------------------|   ----------------High

    Democratic                  |              Democratic

    Morality/                   |              Morality/

    Access                      |              Access

                                |

                                |

                            Low

                            Effectiveness      "OPEN"
```

often result. Such administrations rank low on democratic morality but, other things being equal, tend to be more effective than open administrations.

Of course, no administration is completely open or closed. The "dilemma" is really a continuum (Figure 7.1), with administrations differing in their emphasis of democratic morality and effectiveness values.

The media strategies of the Carter and Reagan presidencies, which are detailed in this and the following chapters, illustrate these value trade-offs. The Carter White House was more open than the Reagan administration. Television coverage of the Iranian hostage crisis contributed heavily to Jimmy Carter's electoral defeat. Ronald Reagan's closed media strategy contributed to his popularity and effectiveness. However, the Reagan administration's successful efforts to restrict coverage isolated the president from the types of questions and criticism that could have prevented the Iran-Contra affair.

JIMMY CARTER AND THE PERILS OF THE OPEN PRESIDENCY

Jody Powell once remarked to a reporter complaining about press access to Ronald Reagan, "Jimmy Carter answered all of your questions every day, and look what happened to him" (Donaldson, 1987: 128). Carter was indeed one of our most open presidents (Locander, 1980). He was also widely perceived as ineffective and unsuccessful (G. Smith, 1986; Hargrove 1988).

Is Jody Powell right? Would Carter have been a more popular and effective president if he had been less accessible? This chapter suggests that Carter's failure to adjust to the demands of the prime-time presidency contributed heavily to his loss of public support and electoral defeat. This was particularly evident in televised coverage of the Iranian hostage crisis.

Accessibility

Jimmy Carter entered the White House determined to "deimperialize" the presidency. He was inaugurated as "Jimmy" instead of "James Earl." Following his inauguration, the Carters walked from the Capitol to the White House. As president, Carter banned high-flown displays of pomp, such as the playing of ruffles and flourishes. Chauffeur service for White House aides and cabinet officers was dropped, and Amy Carter was sent to a predominantly black public school. Carter asked his cabinet to develop plans for staying in touch with the people (Glad, 1980a).

Carter's popularism also extended to the press. ABC's Sam Donaldson writes, "We used to complain about access to Jimmy Carter but compared to access to Ronald Reagan, I was practically one of the Carter family" (Donaldson, 1987:110). In his four years in office, Carter held 59 televised press conferences, as compared with 26 for Ronald Reagan. Unlike Reagan, who avoided uncontrolled encounters with reporters, Carter went out of his way, especially during his first years in office, to be accessible. He also kept his press secretary, Jody Powell, fully informed. Carter (1982:44) writes in his memoirs: "Only rarely in the four years was Jody excluded from my discussion of even the most sensitive issues. The reporters understood this special relationship between us and learned to trust the accuracy of his statements and answers."

Press Naïveté

Despite the media savvy he demonstrated during his campaign, Carter underestimated television's power to shape public opinion, its logistical needs, its commitment to the presidency, and how aggressive the White House press had become in the past decade (Jordan, 1982:379).

For example, soon after he assumed office, Carter decided that he was not going to inform reporters when he left the executive mansion for personal reasons—for example, to go jogging or to take his wife and daughter to the opera or to a museum ("Carter Will Avoid Press on Occasion," 1977). Carter felt these activities had little to do with his official duties and thus were not deserving of coverage. Having revealed himself and his family to the press throughout the campaign, he now wanted some semblance of a personal life.

So Carter's first misstep was that he underestimated the press's commitment to the presidency. Television especially loves human interest stories, particularly during the initial months of a new term. Such coverage is almost always positive, which is why the networks were so surprised by Carter's reaction. Thus, the impression began to be formed that Carter was aloof, arrogant, and perhaps incompetent, as "CBS Evening News" producer Susan Zirinski puts it:

> Jimmy Carter didn't want the constraints of having to alert the press if he wanted to move, so he went jogging at 5:30 in the morning and he didn't even tell us. So if you didn't stake him out you didn't get the jogging. The Carter administration didn't *acknowledge that they had to take a pool with them all the time.* We kept asking and begging, but Jimmy Carter said, "I don't care. If I want to go running, I'm not going to wait for you to get a pool." And that got us mad. We have an arrangement, an agreement. It's part of the job and Carter was terrible.

It is ironic that Carter's second miscalculation was that he was too accessible when it came to coverage of his official duties. Press relations were further aggravated by the Carter administration's failure to restrict access to the president and more thoroughly coordinate press coverage of presidential activities. This has become increasingly necessary as the number of reporters covering the president has ballooned over the years and as television has become the predominant medium covering the chief executive.[3]

The White House is a surprisingly small structure. The Rose Garden, for example, is not much larger than the backyard of an average suburban home. The pressroom has only 48 seats for the approximately 150 reporters and crew who cover the president on a daily basis. This means that reporters often outnumber guests at White House functions. Thus, despite complaints about "stage-managed" news, reporters look to the White House to coordinate coverage, which often means restricting access. Accessibility, however, was a major campaign theme, and Carter did not want to resurrect the image of an isolated president.

Thus, the White House's failure to coordinate coverage of the president hurt the president.

ABC White House cameraman Doug Almond explains:

> A photo-op [opportunity] with the Carter administration was absolute pandemonium. They let everyone in at once and that automatically meant that 25 percent of you would not get the pictures and sound that you had to get. If you have a cabinet meeting, for instance, you have to limit the number of press people allowed in. There are only seven or eight camera positions in the Oval Office. That is it. Once you start letting 15 camerapeople in there, then people have to start fighting for position. The Carter administration would open the doors and you had to go in there like a madman or you got nothing. It turned us into animals. I like the way the Reagan administration has made it more civilized.

This was also true on the road. Almond continues:

> Carter would get out of the car and walk from the motorcade onto the event. You would cover every step because we could get close to him. We got terrific pictures, but it was also absolute mayhem. It was a "cluster-fuck." Imagine a giant cluster of people fucking the president, and each other. He was so wide open. And it didn't do him any good. He should have been more brief. The thing he did wrong from a cameraman's point of view is that he would never back off of a question, and he would answer a question about anything, at anytime. It made it a nightmare to cover the guy, because you could never get off of him. If he said something and you didn't have it on tape, you would be destroyed. That whole scene followed him everywhere he went. If he just let himself get his picture taken, and not answer all those questions, he would have been all right.

Carter's open relationship with the press also caused his administration to "leak" earlier and more profusely than most. Leaks—the unauthorized disclosure of information (usually embarrassing) to the press by the president's staff—are a problem for all administrations. White House aides and cabinet officials, however, feel less inhibited about talking to reporters when the likelihood of a reprimand is low and when a large number of people are involved in the decision process, as was the case since Carter was reluctant to limit the number of people who attended cabinet meetings (Carter, 1982:59–60).

Only three months into the term, for example, *New York Times* correspondent James Wooten wrote an unflattering portrait of Carter that was based on interviews with White House aides. Wooten reported disturbing similarities in the management styles of the president and his hero Hyman G. Rickover, the autocratic architect of the U.S. nuclear submarine fleet. The president, Wooten wrote, "can be brutally brusque and sharp tongued with those who displease him or disagree" (Wooten, 1977:61.) The next day, in a report on the CBS Morning News, Jody Powell candidly remarked, that "I have not made a secret of the fact that this president is not overly given to pats on the back or stroking or a kiss on the ear." (CBS Morning News, April 26, 1977). These stories were damaging to Carter because they came so early in his term, at a time when the public and the press were forming their first impressions of the new president.

Response to Negative Coverage

Carter also failed to develop a comprehensive strategy for combating television's built-in bias toward negative coverage. For example, as we saw earlier, television news requires simplicity. As a candidate, the campaign forced Carter to refine and hone his message of moral leadership. It was a simple message and Carter stuck to it, despite criticism that he take more specific stands on the issues. As president, however, his remarks tended to be long, complicated, and as befitted an engineer, somewhat dry.[4]

In his first televised message, for example, Carter set forth an economic stimulus package—as well as proposals to set up an energy department, a tax rebate, government reorganization, reductions in government red tape, and zero-based budgeting. In contrast, Ronald Reagan in his first speech to the nation deliberately "zeroed in on a single theme—uncontrolled government spending had sapped America's economic vitality and forced the urgent need to shift to a new approach to tame inflation" (H. Smith, 1981:23).

Similarly, Carter failed to televise, and thereby capitalize on, his achievements. Carter naively assumed that the press would mirror his performance in office and that voters would reward hard work and substantive achievements. He also felt that voters and the press would belittle image-building activities (Hargrove, 1988:231). Consequently, he ignored advice given to him at the outset of his term to "give the public visible signals it needs to understand what is happening" (H. Johnson, 1980:142). So impressive feats such as the passage of the Panama Canal treaties, the overhaul of the civil service system, the enactment of a comprehensive energy program, the successful negotiation of the second Strategic Arms Limitation Treaty (SALT II), the formalization of relations with the People's Republic of China, and the Camp David accords did not stick in the public mind because insufficient care was given to their visual presentation. A year and a half would pass before Carter hired media man Gerald Rafshoon. By then the negative image of Carter had set in and was difficult to dispel (Wooten, 1979).

By temperament and conviction, Jimmy Carter was poorly suited to the prime-time presidency. The size of the corps requires all presidents to coordinate coverage and limit press access, but Carter declined. As Powell put it, the Reagan administration "cut severely into the flow of information and manage[d] it with a much firmer hand than we were able or willing to do" (Hertsgaard, 1988:8).

Television requires "sound-bite" simplicity, but Carter gave complicated responses to reporters' questions and presented to the nation an unwieldy legislative agenda. Television requires lead time, but Carter liked to be spontaneous, as when he appeared at the Kennedy Center without first notifying the press. Television requires visible indicators of success on a regular basis, but Carter's major accomplishments—the release of the hostages, the Israeli-Egypt peace accords, the Panama Canal treaties—were won by Carter acting alone, personally, and in private. Carter was given high marks for his performance during the Camp David negotiations as he "sat for endless hours listening to each side, then led each of them one more step down the path to agreement" (Salinger, 1981:32) Patience, however, is not photogenic. Nowhere is this more apparent than in television coverage of the Iran hostage crisis.

THE IRAN HOSTAGE CRISIS

Television coverage of the Iran hostage crisis illustrates the media's power to shape public opinion as well as the adverse impact TV news can have on the presidency. Although an extreme and somewhat unique case, an analysis of television coverage of the hostage crisis highlights many of television's most serious shortcomings, which are less tangible—though still present—in routine coverage of the presidency.

Background

The shah of Iran had been an important ally of the United States since 1953, when the Central Intelligence Agency (CIA) helped return him to power (G. Smith, 1986:180–207). The shah insured that a steady supply of oil would flow through the Persian Gulf to the West. He also made Iran an important bulwark against possible Soviet intervention in the Middle East, as well as an excellent overseas customer. In return, the United States helped ward off both foreign and domestic threats to the Pahlevi dynasty. The United States sold the shah sophisticated weapons that made Iran a formidable military power. CIA-trained "SAVAK" agents imprisoned and tortured suspected dissidents. And a succession of presidents, even though they were aware of the shah's horrible record on human rights, reiterated U.S. support for the shah. Even Carter, who made human rights a top foreign policy priority, gave a stirring and emotional toast to the shah in which he said that Iran was "an island of stability in one of the more troubled areas of the world" and that this was due to "the respect and the admiration and love which" the Iranian people gave the shah (Salinger, 1981:6).

In fact, most Iranians detested the shah's authoritarian rule, his Western-style reforms, and the torture he had inflicted on his political opponents. In 1978, a popular uprising forced the shah to flee Iran.

Unknown to the world, the shah had terminal cancer, and shortly after leaving Iran he requested permission to enter the United States for medical treatment. Carter, under pressure from the shah's good friends David Rockefeller and Henry Kissinger, as well as his own Secretary of State, reluctantly agreed to let the shah enter a New York hospital. This decision enraged student militants in Tehran, and on November 4, 1979, they stormed the U.S. embassy and took 66 prisoners. Fifty-two were kept prisoner for 444 days. All were released minutes after Ronald Reagan was sworn in as president.

Extensive Coverage

No single incident was as widely chronicled by television as the taking of the U.S. embassy and its occupants (G. Smith, 1986:198). During the first six months of the crisis, the networks devoted up to a third of their nightly news programs to the Iran story. Two thirds was not uncommon in times of increased drama. The three networks spent a combined total of approximately $1 million a day covering the Iran story (Adams and Heyl, 1981:26; Hill, 1980; Said, 1981:29).

Never before had a network anchorman counted off the days of a foreign policy crisis.[5] Never before had as many "specials" been aired about a single subject (Hill, 1981). ABC News created an entire news program: "The Iran Crisis: America Held Hostage." The program boosted ABC News' generally lackluster ratings to competitive levels and was transformed into "Nightline" on March 24, 1980, because its ratings rivaled those of the "Tonight Show with Johnny Carson" (Altheide, 1980b:29).

Television gave unprecedented attention to the hostage crisis despite the fact that Iran posed no physical threat to the United States and despite the fact that most foreign policy professionals felt that the Soviet's invasion of Afghanistan and the Iran-Iraq war were far more important to the national interest (G. Smith, 1986).

Why? In addition to meeting any reasonable standard of newsworthiness, Adams and Heyl (1981:29) argue that the hostage story was particularly well suited to television: It had a human interest and humanitarian dimension; it had conflict, drama, and good pictures; it had symbolic appeal; and it involved the president. Moreover, new technologies had made Iran instantly accessible.

> Night after night, for over fourteen months the networks spotlighted chanting Iranian mobs, cautious U.S. spokesmen, stoic hostage families, sundry international courts and commissions, candles and yellow ribbons, staged tapes of hostages, insistent Iranian spokesmen, Christmas and Easter with the hostages, a failed rescue attempt, rumors and endless speculation. . . . Iran had it all: straightforward and fundamental conflict between two sides; a powerful elementary theme (what is or will be happening to the hostages?) good footage of worried families, the earnest President, the bearded Ayatollah, and even sometimes-blindfolded hostages themselves; action pictures of angry crowds in Iran and in the United States; adding up to a continuing, suspenseful, telegenic narrative of nationwide appeal. [Adams and Heyl, 1981:25]

Negative Coverage

Although extensive, news coverage of Iran was far from comprehensive. Critics have charged that coverage was driven more by a desire for high ratings than a desire to serve democracy, more by a desire to entertain rather than to inform, and more by a desire to arouse rather than educate. Former Undersecretary of State George Ball referred to television's coverage of the crisis as "the greatest soap opera of the year" (Nimmo and Combs, 1985:144).

In his comprehensive study of TV coverage of the hostage crisis, Altheide (1981b) concluded that the networks' coverage of the Iran story was "oversimplified and underexplained." Altheide argues that the networks lavished attention on the plight of the hostages, world reaction to the embassy takeover, the hostages' families, and Iranian students in the United States but virtually ignored the story's historical, political, and particularly, religious context. Little attention, for example, was paid to the role the United States played in bringing the shah to power, keeping him in power, and the nature of life in Iran under the shah's rule. Such information, Altheide argues, was critical to an understanding of the revolution and the taking of the hostages. With no rational basis to justify their actions, the Iranian people and the followers of Ayatollah Khomeini were portrayed as "confused, insane, or just plain stupid" (1981a:29).

The networks' need for good visuals also led to an emphasis on crowds of chanting students outside the embassy gates. Such scenes were included in 80 percent of the film from Tehran (Altheide, 1981a). What the American people did not see, however, was that just a couple of blocks away from the embassy life in Tehran proceeded more or less as usual.

At home, television extensively covered Iranian students who were involved in demonstrations, particularly when they turned violent. Students who did not support the taking of hostages, however, received little attention. The scope and intensity of the crisis were magnified as the networks rapidly cut from foreign to domestic reports, which conjured up the image that all of the United States was under attack at home and abroad (Altheide, 1981a). Interviews with the suffering hostages and their families further dramatized the coverage.[6]

Emboldened Reporters

To the consternation of the Carter administration and State Department officials, television reporters and anchors took on the role of media diplomats. The fact that none of them spoke Farsi and that none of them were experts in Iranian affairs did not prevent them from speculating about future actions by principal actors (Raphel, 1981–82). CBS reported that "draconian measures" may be necessary to curtail oil consumption, even though at the time the United States imported only 4 percent of its oil from Iran (Nimmo and Combs, 1985:155). And ABC's Sam Donaldson warned Iran that force would be used if the hostages were harmed, although no one in the Carter administration had publicly suggested that the military option was being considered:

> Not withstanding such constraint, it is understood here and ought to be understood in Iran, that, if any harm does come to the Americans, the president will not hesitate to order an appropriate American military response. [Altheide, 1981a:153]

Impact on Public Opinion

At home, the plight of the hostages captured the nation's attention more than any international crisis since the bombing of Pearl Harbor. The networks had given scant attention to Iran up until the hostage crisis, an average of just over five minutes a year from 1972 to 1977 (Altheide, 1981b). Thus, most Americans had little or no context in which to place the events that were being revealed to them on television. Coverage, on the whole, did not increase the American public's appreciation of why the crisis occurred nor the complexities involved in getting the hostages released.

Instead, television presented an extensive, superficial, simplistic, truncated, exaggerated, and melodramatic version of what was happening in Iran, and the American people responded accordingly. The nation became preoccupied with the problem. Others were angry, frustrated, and restless. Crowds taunted and attacked Iranian students in major cities. Transport workers refused to service Iranian airplanes, and longshoremen refused to unload Iranian ships. Many Americans, including members of Congress, demanded a military response. Many more grew impatient with the Carter administration's lack of progress in getting the hostages released (Nimmo and Combs, 1985:147).

The question arises, Would the American people have become as aroused if they had simply read accounts of the crisis in their local paper, as opposed to watching it night after night on television? Consider the case of the *Pueblo*, which is similar to the hostage crisis in many respects except for the fact that it received far less TV coverage (Altheide, 1981b:28).

The *Pueblo*

On January 23, 1968, North Korea captured the *Pueblo*, a small navy electronics surveillance ship that had wandered, in North Korea's opinion, too close to its coast. The 82 civilian and military crew were held by the North Koreans for 11 months. Torture was inflicted regularly, and one crew member died. Tension between the United States and the Koreans was running high. Just prior to the *Pueblo*'s capture, the United States had warned North Korea about stepped-up infiltration of South Korea (Brandt, 1969). Thus, there was a genuine fear that the crisis could escalate into an armed conflict between the United States and North Korea and perhaps the Soviet Union.

Despite the story's importance, however, the *Pueblo* received about a fifth the amount of coverage by television news as the hostage crisis. Weeks went by without a single story from Korea. In contrast, the networks aired no fewer than 33 stories a month about the hostages in Tehran (Altheide, 1981b:28). The fact that Iran was more accessible to the foreign press and that new technologies (satellites and minicameras) had made it cheaper and more convenient for the networks to cover the hostage story are two of the factors that account for the different levels of coverage.

Impact on the Carter Administration

No argument is made here that television's presence extended the crisis. It took about the same amount of time to get the *Pueblo* crew released as it did to get the hostages out of Iran. The *Pueblo* crisis, however, was far less wrenching to the nation and far less injurious to the president (Ranney, 1983; Cutler, 1984). Those differences can be attributed to television news. Television news coverage of the Iran crisis affected the presidency in the following ways.

First, television news *personalized* the crisis. Johnson was able to distance himself from the *Pueblo* crisis and was eventually able to turn the problem over to the State Department. Thus, a crisis became an ongoing foreign policy problem. As the nation's crisis manager, Carter was involved in the initial steps to free the hostages. Nevertheless, when it was clear that the crisis would not be resolved quickly, television made it awkward for Carter to distance himself from it.

Second, television news *exaggerated* the crisis. Not nearly as many people were as conscious of and as concerned about the fate of the *Pueblo* crew as were conscious of and concerned about the fate of the hostages in Iran. Television captured the nation's attention and focused it on the hostages and the president's inability to get them released. Moreover, as media analyst Edward Epstein and others have pointed out, because a significant portion of the audience for the three network evening news programs "flows through" from the program preceding it, television news inadvertently exposes large numbers of viewers to subjects that they ordinarily would not be interested in or care much about (Epstein, 1973a). Thus, once the problem was nationalized, it was more difficult to resolve.

According to President Carter, the Iranian militants agreed to release the hostages if the following demands were met: first, that the shah be returned; second, that the United States apologize to the world for alleged crimes against the Iranian people; and third, that financial damages and the shah's assets be paid over to Iran. Carter says he refused to give serious consideration to "any" of these demands because to do so would have "besmirched the nation's honor" (Carter, 1982:467).

However, had the crisis not been as extensively covered, it is likely that the nation's honor would not have played as great a role. In the case of the *Pueblo*, for example, U.S. negotiators admitted that the *Pueblo* had been spying on North Korea, agreed that the *Pueblo* had been seized by the North Koreans as an act of self-defense; apologized to the North Koreans for this infraction, and requested that the Democratic People's Republic of Korea deal "leniently" with the *Pueblo*'s crew (Brandt, 1969:228). Had the *Pueblo* crisis been more extensively covered, it is likely that such a resolution would have been politically unacceptable in the United States. (The "confession" was repudiated as soon as the crew was safely returned.)

U.S. Apology to North Korea

The Government of the United States of America, acknowledging the validity of the confessions of the crew of the USS "Pueblo" and of the documents of evidence produced by the representative of the Government of the Democratic People's Republic of Korea to the effect that the ship, which was seized by the self-defense measures of the naval vessels of the Korean People's Army in the territorial waters of the Democratic People's Republic of Korea on many occasions and conducted espionage activities of spying out important military and state secrets of the Democratic People's Republic of Korea.

Shoulders full Responsibility and solemnly apologizes for the grave acts of espionage committed by the U.S. ship against the Democratic People's Republic of Korea after having intruded into the territorial waters of the Democratic People's Republic of Korea,

And gives firm assurance that no U.S. ships will intrude again in the future into the territorial waters of the Democratic People's Republic of Korea.

Meanwhile, the Government of the United States of America earnestly requests the Government of the Democratic People's Republic of Korea to deal leniently with the former crew members of the USS "Pueblo" confiscated by the Democratic People's Republic of Korea side, taking into consideration the fact that these crew members have confessed honestly to their crimes and petitioned the Government of the People's Republic for leniency.

Simultaneous with the signing of this document, the undersigned acknowledges receipt of 82 crew members of the USS "Pueblo" and one corpse.

On behalf of the Government of the United States of America,

Gilbert H. Woodward
Major General, United States Army
23 Dec., 1968[7]

In addition, television exaggerated the president's ability to resolve the crisis. Implicit in the coverage was the assumption that the presidency had the resources to get the hostages out of Tehran—if he would just stand firm. Extensive coverage, by its very nature, leads people to think that the president has more power than he actually has (If he is not that powerful, why otherwise would he be covered that much?). This tendency by citizens to exaggerate the power of the presidency is reinforced by television's bias toward coverage of presidential actions and command decisions more than the constraints on presidential action.

Third, television news *accelerated* the evaluation of the president's performance. Most foreign policy professionals have concluded that the events in Iran were beyond U.S. control and that there was little any president could have done to free the hostages any sooner (Hargrove, 1988:256). Nevertheless, by focusing on the problem, the television networks increased the pressure on Carter to find a solution, fast. Carter took a variety of actions to force the Iranians to release the hostages. He froze Iranian assets held in U.S. banks, impounded U.S. land owned by Iranians, discontinued oil purchases from Iran, and brought the matter before the United Nations Security Council and the World Bank. In addition, he marshaled support for these actions by our allies, and he pursued negotiations with the captors. At one point he even threatened the ayatollah with military action if the hostages were harmed (Carter, 1982).

Finally, television news coverage of the hostage crisis *frustrated* the president. Carter received little "credit" for his efforts to free the hostages because, by and large, they could not be shown in pictures—nor could the complexity of the negotiating process and the logistical difficulties involved in getting the hostages released. Instead, descriptions of these efforts had to compete with vivid pictures—shown many times over—of angry Iranian students burning the U.S. flag.

Caught between a stubborn ayatollah and a public that had been whipped into a frenzy by the networks, a frustrated Carter made a series of controversial decisions. He expelled Iranian students whose visas had expired. He also forbade demonstrations by Iranians on federal property. Both orders raised serious legal and constitutional questions concerning the president's power to limit free speech. Carter also approved a rescue mission that ended in disaster, resulting in the only deaths associated with his administration as well as the resignation of Secretary of State Cyrus Vance, who opposed the plan. Vance's resignation highlighted the deep divisions within the administration, a story line that received much attention by the networks.

Carter's Response

Despite the negative impact that television coverage of the Iran hostage crisis had on his administration, Carter maintained an open presidency. Following the failed rescue attempt, Carter did want to pressure reporters to leave Tehran but declined after Powell reminded him that a direct order would "arouse charges of news management" (Holmes, 1986:63). In fact, many observers felt Carter and his aides were far too accessible to the press and that they handled the ayatollah far better than they handled the news media. By continuing to respond to press queries, Carter elevated the story's importance and unwittingly lent support for a greater commitment by the networks to the story. This, in turn, created greater pressure for Carter to secure the hostages' freedom (Hargrove, 1988:256). When asked in a 1986 interview what he would have done differently, Hodding Carter III, spokesman for the State Department, responded in kind:

> Me? I would have shut up. Absolutely. I wouldn't have had me out there every day. At the time I thought we were doing the right thing. It was terrible coverage. It is terrible when you allow yourself to get into the position of: There are the bad mobs in the street, there is a slightly crazed, fanatical Khomeini, here's the government spokesman, and here's our story. And that's what the story came down to. That's not journalism, for God's sake, that's theater. I would have shut the spokesman up. I'd say, There's nothing new to say on it. We're not going to engage in this game, thank you. It would have taken it off the (front) pages and off the television and into the arena it belonged—private negotiations. [Keebler, 1986:5]

CONCLUSION

Carter's commitment to an open administration made him particularly vulnerable to the adverse consequences of the six o'clock presidency. In addition to the impact of extensive negative coverage, which he was unable and unwilling to counteract, televised coverage of the hostage crisis was particularly harmful to Carter because it occurred during the presidential reassessment season of his administration. With the presidential campaign in full swing, the press's attention naturally turned to the question of whether Carter would/should be returned to office. Thus, it is arguably the case that had the crisis occurred earlier in the president's term—during the personal profile or legislative agenda seasons—when the press's docket was full, the Iran story would not have been as intensively covered.

Many of the themes that tied the networks' coverage of the hostage crisis fitted well into the presidential reassessment season. The president who was weak and ineffective in handling the economy, and weak and ineffective in fending off potential rivals within his own party, was also weak and ineffective in dealing with this small, barbaric nation. Unfortunately, election day fell on the one-year anniversary of the crisis, and the networks ran long stories that recapped the hostage crisis. Voters were once again reminded of the hostages' continued captivity and Carter's inability to get them released. Ronald Reagan was elected; the hostages were released on Inauguration Day. The mistakes Jimmy Carter made in his handling of the media were not lost on the new administration. But even the Reagan administration was not immune to the adverse consequences of the six o'clock presidency.

NOTES

1. Carter quote from "CBS Evening News with Walter Cronkite." Transcript. April 20, 1977, p. 6.

2. Powell quote from in "Meeting the Press: A Conversation with David Gergen and Jody Powell" (1982:10).

3. Historian Betty Glad (1980a:502) suggests that Carter's effectiveness diminished as he faced more distinguished and more skeptical audiences:

> As president . . . his formal addresses to Congress and to the people have shown a stiff quality. Indeed, Carter has two speaking styles. With blacks, children, the "people"—the powerless—Carter is at the height of his emotional spontaneity and warmth. But before larger, more prestigious audiences, such as the American Bar Association and the Chicago Council on Foreign Relations, or in situations where he might lose, Carter is likely to hide behind the facts and figures and a monotone.

4. Paradoxically, Carter was also prone to alarmist and exaggerated rhetoric. For example, he called the Soviet invasion of Afghanistan the greatest threat to world peace since World War II. Gaddis Smith (1986:245) says that such rhetoric diluted the power of Carter's words and his ability to persuade.

5. As Walter Cronkite did when he concluded each broadcast: "And that's the way it is, January 19, 1981, the 443rd day Americans have been held in Iran."

6. As Altheide (1981a:142) notes:

> The family reaction . . . was always available for a feature story on holidays, or for a quick reaction to a move by the White House or by the Iranians. Holiday stories were particularly noteworthy, since one or more family members could be shown on film to be crying, or emotionally drained. . . . (The self-proclaimed role of at least one network, ABC, to console Americans over the hostage situation was apparent when the Christmas Eve newscast presented nearly five minutes of Luciano Pavarotti singing "Ave Maria.")

7. From Armbister (1971:340).

8

The Sound-Bite Presidency

You don't tell us how to stage the news,
and we won't tell you how to cover it.
                            From the desk of Larry Speakes,
                            Press Secretary to Ronald Reagan[1]

A plaque on Press Secretary Larry Speakes' desk summarized the Reagan administration's approach to press relations. Convinced that the press had contributed to the decline and fall of Jimmy Carter (as well as Johnson, Nixon, and Ford), Ronald Reagan and his aides resolved that their presidency would not suffer a similar fate (Weisman, 1984:35). To govern effectively, they believed it was imperative that they dominate the press. No president in this century took fewer questions from the press, held fewer press conferences, kept reporters at a greater distance, exerted more control over the flow of information, or used television more ingeniously than Ronald Reagan. Such tactics contributed to Reagan's enormous popularity. His media strategy, however, crippled and almost destroyed his administration. This was a closed administration.

Figure 8.1
Controlled and Uncontrolled Electronic Media

Controlled and Uncontrolled Electronic Media

MOST			LEAST
CONTROLLED..CONTROLLED			

Presidential	Party	Debate	Evening News
Address	Convention		
Political			
Advertisements			
Radio	Press		
	Conference		

IMPORTANCE OF TELEVISION

Television's wide reach, immediacy, and potential for influencing public opinion made it the focal point of the Reagan administration's media strategy (Deaver, 1987:147). To appreciate the Reagan response to the six o'clock presidency, it is necessary to distinguish "controlled" from "uncontrolled" television. The White House has the most influence over controlled television's portrayal of the president. The tone of such coverage is generally positive, but this can vary, depending on the personal attributes of the president and the skills of his staff. Examples of controlled television include presidential addresses and political advertisements. Toward the other end of the continuum is the least controlled media, principally the evening news. The White House can exert some influence over the president's schedule, access to the president and his aides, and the release of information. However, most administrations have not been able to significantly influence the tone of the coverage the president receives on the evening news over an extended period of time. Arrayed along the continuum lie the other forms of coverage, their position based on the level of control the White House has over the president's portrayal.

THE TWO RONALD REAGANS

In their desire to use controlled television to rally support for the president and his policies, the president's media aides faced a problem: In controlled settings, Ronald Reagan was indeed the Great Communicator. This was a man who had spent virtually his entire adult life before the camera and the microphone. In uncontrolled settings, however, the president often made incredibly inaccurate and politically devastating statements. This "other" Ronald Reagan has been referred to by one author as the "Amiable Dunce" (Hertsgaard, 1988). The media strategy his aides devised had to showcase the president's unparalleled talent in controlled settings. At the same time, it had to compensate for his poor performance in uncontrolled settings. Let us consider these two Ronald Reagans.

The Great Communicator

Few presidents were as well suited to the electronic presidency as Ronald Reagan. Lyndon Johnson's personal magnetism did not transmit over the airwaves; Nixon's awkwardness was accentuated by television's hot lights; Ford's and Carter's shrill and garbled speech did not make for easy listening. But Ronald Reagan was the quintessential televised president. He was poised in a medium others found menacing. His voice was clear and well modulated. As a favorite after-dinner speaker and public relations personality for General Electric, Reagan had learned to charm a wide variety of audiences. Commenting on one of his early televised addresses, columnist Hedrick Smith wrote that, in pointed contrast to Carter, "Reagan zeroed in on a single theme . . . and with folksy examples and informality, drew his audience into his way of thinking. . . . [I]n tone and style he seemed closer to Roosevelt's fireside chats" than Carter, who had tried to evoke the famous fireside chats in a speech on the energy crisis by sitting near a fireplace in a cardigan sweater (H. Smith, 1981:23).

The president's considerable talents are illustrated by David Gergen, who was director of communications during the first Reagan administration. On April 29, 1982, Reagan gave a televised speech defending his 1983 budget and economic plan. Budget negotiations between the White House and a bipartisan group from Congress were at a standstill, and the president was appealing to the nation for support for his cuts. A chart depicting the size of the federal deficit under different budget scenarios was next to his desk. A felt-tip pen lay nearby. The plan was for the president to draw a line showing the anticipated deficits under a new compromise proposal that the president supported.

The run-through during the afternoon went fine. Unfortunately, someone forgot to put the cap back on the marker, which dried out by the time the speech was to air. The president began the speech. But when he got to the part where he needed to use the marker, nothing came out. Realizing what was wrong, the president kept on going:

Our original cuts totaled $101 billion. They—I can't make a big enough mark to show you—but they were rejected, believe me. Our own representatives from the Congress proposed compromises at $60 billion. Their counterparts from the Democratic side of the aisle proposed 35. ["Transcript of President's Address," 1982:A16]

An astute aide grabbed another marker, removed its cap, got down on his hands and knees (so as to be out of camera range), and—as the Secret Service stared incredulously—crawled over to the president. Without skipping a beat or losing eye contact with the audience, the president reached down with one hand, took the new marker, and continued:

In our meeting yesterday, which went on for more than three hours, our compromise of $60 billion was rejected. Now my pen is working. And then I swallowed hard and volunteered to split the difference between our $60 and their $35, and settle for $48.

The Amiable Dunce

Although unsurpassed in his ability to read from a prepared script, the president did not fare well in less-controlled settings, such as press conferences and other presentations to reporters. His knowledge of his administration's most important policies and actions, for example, remained weak throughout his presidency (Regan, 1988). This often led to ghastly misstatements of fact that often caused considerable embarrassment to the administration. For example, on one occasion the president claimed that 80 percent of the nation's air pollution was caused by trees; on another, that many homeless people prefer to sleep in the gutter rather than in government-sponsored shelters.

So on a daily basis, the administration's reliance on the evening news programs to get its message across to the American people had to compensate for Reagan's shortcomings as well as the networks' desire to profile them extensively.

RESPONSE TO EXTENSIVE COVERAGE

Fearing that television's obsession with the presidency would overexpose the gaffe-prone president, access to the president was severely curtailed: Reagan (first term) held half as many press conferences as Carter. Reporters were also kept at a much greater physical distance from this president. This was easier to justify after the assassination attempt on his life. (The press corps has grown so large that infiltration by an assassin is a genuine security risk.) But this was also done to protect Reagan from the reporters' questions (Donaldson, 1987). When reporters were able to get close, they seldom got responses to their queries.

For example, in 1982 the White House decided to prohibit questions during photo opportunities and to limit the number of correspondents accompanying the cameramen to one per network. They argued that the Oval Office was not large enough to accommodate more. This resulted in the rather unusual and downright eerie scene that I witnessed in which the president and his guest sat in silence for approximately 20 minutes as the sound of motor drives filled the air like a swarm of locusts. Every once in a while a reporter would ignore the restrictions and ask a question of the president or his guest. "No questions" was the response from the press secretary, as the president and his guest continued to pose for the cameras and chat among themselves. When the president did respond during photo opportunities or other occasions, his answers gave only minimal access to his thoughts and intentions (Weisman, 1984). As former Chief of Staff Donald Regan has written:

> Every moment of every public appearance was scheduled, every word was scripted, every place where Reagan was expected to stand was chalked with toe marks. The President was always being prepared for a performance, and this had the inevitable effect of preserving him from confrontation and the genuine interplay of opinion, question, and argument that form the basis of decision. [Regan, 1988:248]

Nor did this White House hesitate to shut reporters out completely when it felt the need. The White House gave an overly optimistic account of the president's condition following the assassination attempt, which reporters were prevented from verifying (Diamond, 1981). A press "blackout" was ordered at the Reykjavik summit with the Soviets. Aware of television's impact on public support for the Vietnam War, the White House barred reporters from covering the invasion of Grenada (Deaver, 1987). Virtually the only access reporters had to the president was when he walked to or from an event or when he walked across the White House lawn to his helicopter. Here the president gave what Buchanan (1987:123) calls the "cupped ear" interview:

> As the president moved from the White House to a waiting helicopter on the lawn, he would pause briefly to answer questions shouted by reporters cordoned off some distance away. With the din of the propeller whirring deliberately in the background, he would cup his ear as if straining to hear the question. He was then free to answer forthrightly, answer a question other than the one posed or strike an amiable, "Sorry, I can't hear" posture and stride off with a smile.

RESPONSES TO NEGATIVE COVERAGE

A variety of tactics were also used to respond to television's built-in negativity. The Reagan press office began by quite literally putting reporters in their place. Hard-liners within the administration insisted that the press be moved out of the White House pressroom so that the president would not have to walk past them each morning on his way to the Oval Office. Instead, the pressroom was refurbished, and the comfortable couches and stuffed chairs left over from the informal Carter years were replaced with plastic chairs that were bolted to the floor. The hope was that the more formal surroundings would encourage greater decorum among reporters (Powell, 1984). The White House also prohibited reporters and their crews from relaxing on the White House lawn outside the pressroom—a favorite resting place from crowded working conditions. That the press had to pass through a metal detector and have their belongings inspected each time they entered the grounds—although no reporter has ever physically attacked a president, and in fact the corps has acted as a buffer against such an attack—served as a potent reminder of the administration's desire for control (Donaldson, 1987). In addition, Reagan's press secretary, Larry Speakes, was not kept nearly as well informed as former press secretary Jody Powell. Correspondent Leslie Stahl points out:

> The basic difference between the Carter and Reagan administrations is that Jody Powell was plugged in and Larry Speakes is not. For most reporters, the day consisted of following Jody Powell around. We draped ourselves outside his office. A lot of reporters thought it was a waste of time to get on the phone because Jody Powell knew everything anyway; so if you could get to him, you could find out what you wanted to find out. I'm on the phone more now, trying to get to someone who has answers, because Larry doesn't.

The White House also tried to woo a select group of reporters for informal question-and-answer sessions over cocktails. "The beauty of the device, according to the Administration, was that it created an atmosphere that inhibited tough questioning and encouraged empathy with the president's point of view. Even an ardent critic might be expected to feel an obligation to a friendly couple like the Reagans after having accepted their hospitality and basked in their charm" (Buchanan, 1987:123).

Aides also restyled the press conferences to better suit their president. Most press conferences were held during prime time (unlike Carter's, which were held during the afternoon). The aim here was to avoid reports and commentaries on the network evening news shows that spotlighted presidential mistakes and stumbles and ignored those parts of the conference in which the president performed well (Weisman, 1984:73). Reagan's advantage was strengthened by requiring the unusually unruly corps to remain seated, to avoid shouting, and to raise their hands in order to be recognized (Deaver, 1987).

The White House took full advantage of the size of the prime-time audience by exploiting the White House's telegenic qualities. Viewers saw a tall, slim, and trim president—a man who looked to many how a president ought to look—stride briskly down a long hallway to the East Room. The "ceremonial extravagances, the red carpet and chandeliers . . . [gave] the public a false impression of conviviality and shared purpose, with Mr. Reagan joking and calling on reporters by their first names—in some cases reporters he has never met" (Weisman, 1984:73). Several reporters contributed to the festive atmosphere that the White House encouraged by wearing outrageous clothing—bright-red sports jackets and blouses (supposedly Nancy's favorite color)—to capture the president's attention.

"DISPOSABLE" LIEUTENANTS

To deflect negative coverage, the Reagan staff used other people as lightning rods to deflect high-voltage criticism from the president. James Watt, for example, Secretary of Interior, drastically weakened his department's traditional role as environmental watchdog. Reagan supported his deemphasis of conservation policies in favor of those that bolstered the economy (Shabecoff, 1983). Under his leadership, public resources set aside by previous administrations were made available for economic development. Watt opened large portions of the Outer Continental shelf and vast areas of public lands to oil and coal companies. He promoted oil and gas drilling in federal wilderness areas. Watt was the first Secretary of Interior to oppose expansion of the national parks.

Most of Watt's new policies did not require action by the president. Thus, it was Watt who bore the brunt of the political fallout from environmental and other groups, who waged an intense political war against him. Ill will was fostered by Watt when he banned the Beach Boys from performing at July 4th ceremonies at the Washington Monument. Watts' comment that his coal advisory committee had "a black, a woman, two Jews and a cripple" led to his resignation in October 1983.

It is very unlikely that Watt intentionally made these particular remarks to draw attention to himself and away from his controversial policies. But it was his intention to deflect political pressure away from the president, even if it cost him his job. Watt told the president upon taking the job that if he was successful in implementing the president's policies, the political pressure would be so great that he would have to be fired after 18 months (Watt, 1985:198). When Watt resigned, the "problem" at Interior was over. The press's attention shifted to other topics. The president's controversial policies, however, remained intact. On other occasions they made sure to shield Reagan from the effects of negative coverage. Office of Management and Budget director David Stockman, and later Health and Human Services secretary Richard Schweiker, took the political heat when a public outcry greeted the president's proposed cuts in Social Security payments (Hertsgaard, 1988:122).

INJECTING HAPPY NEWS

The Reagan White House also attempted to deflect negative coverage by injecting "happy news" into the networks' daily agenda. The president was encouraged by his staff to use his friendly personality to defuse hostile questions from reporters (Kirschten, 1984:154). Palentz and Guthrie (1985) examined coverage of the president and found that in over 90 percent of the televised images of the president Reagan was shown as smiling, affable, and naturally buoyant (also see Meer, 1986). Surprise birthday parties for the president were thrown (while the cameras were rolling) during a press briefing, and other "spontaneous" upbeat events were staged (e.g., scenes of the president eating at McDonald's, riding on horseback, chopping wood, and "pumping" iron) to lighten the critical reporting that aides felt characterized much of the networks' coverage.

INCREASED GOVERNMENT SECRECY

These are some of the most obvious examples of the Reagan Administration's attempt to manipulate press coverage. They were reinforced by other, less publicized, efforts by Reagan appointees to severely restrict the flow of information from the executive branch. Such information could be a potential source of negative coverage of the president. In a lengthy article published in *Harper's*, Walter Karp (1985) detailed these efforts:

- The Reagan administration sought to weaken the Freedom of Information Act (FOIA), which reporters have used to wrench information from governmental bureaucracies.

- The Reagan administration also cut back on the publication of government documents (such as comparisons of U.S. and Soviet military capabilities), which the media frequently relies on to challenge presidential statements and government policies.

- To avoid having to comply with the public meetings requirement of the Advisory Committee Act, the White House structured key advisory panels to exclude the public and the press from oversight of federal rule-making proceedings.

- The president expanded executive privilege to include the entire executive branch, not just conversations in the Oval Office.

- The president signed Executive Order 12356, which placed greater restrictions on the declassification of government documents.

- The Reagan administration adopted regulations that required government officials with access to intelligence information to clear with the government any materials concerning national security that they wish to publish or present.

- In March 1983 the president signed an executive order that made all federal employees with access to classified information subject to lie-detector tests.

RESPONSE TO THEMATIC COVERAGE

Nowhere was the White House's knowledge of television news put to more productive use than in the orchestration of thematic coverage of the president. Reagan's media advisers understood that thematic coverage was one of television's most distinguishing features. Thus, they sought to influence the networks' news agenda daily and over an extended period of time (and thereby counteract the "four seasons" dynamic). Thematic coverage was reinforced by "line of the day" and "theme of the week" strategies as well as the sophisticated exploitation of television's dependence on pictures.

Line of the Day

Top aides met each morning to agree on a "line of the day"—an agreed-on response—that they would push during formal and informal encounters with reporters. The agreed-on line was also put "on line," where it could be instantly accessed by top officials via a computer terminal. Conference calls to lower-echelon press spokesmen in the federal bureaucracy got the line of the day out to the rest of the bureaucracy. Mark Hertsgaard (1988:36) reported a typical line of the day conversation in his book *On Bended Knee*:

It was like, "Okay what do we say about Lebanon today?" We'd go through the newspapers and see a story about South Africa, say, and figure out how we wanted to handle that. "Well, no comment it," we'd decide, or "That's a Pentagon story, we will shut up. State, you've got the lead today on George Shultz's press conference in Brazil." Now, the White House may say, "Look, the President's got a statement tomorrow, so shut up today goddammit, just shut up. Don't preempt the President. We'll cut your nuts off if you leak anything out on this one," that kind of guidance. Other times we would say, "Here's what we're going to say, everybody just say it at once. I don't care if you're asked the question or not, everybody in the administration today praises Gemayel's leadership, or Mubarak's leadership, or whatever it is."

The line of the day served several purposes. First, it was meant to curb the tendency for aides to leak disparate lines to push White House policy in a desired direction. Second, the line of the day was meant to set the press agenda for the day, by focusing coverage on topics the White House wanted highlighted and away from those they did not. Finally, the line of the day was meant to shift the tone of coverage from negative to neutral—and if possible, to positive. These efforts were supplemented by the "spin patrol"—a moniker attached to aides who spent several hours each day trying to get reporters and producers to put the desired interpretation ("spin") on their stories (Kirschten, 1984). The theme of the week was an extension of the line of the day strategy in which the White House would address only briefly, if at all, queries that did not directly relate to subjects that the White House wanted spotlighted.

Use of Visuals

The Reagan staff believed that they had to control television's pictures in order to win over the public. How the president looked was as important, often more important, as what he accomplished or set out to accomplish. This White House was particularly adept at exploiting television's dependence on pictures, as Michael Deaver, the president's chief media aide, explained in his book *Behind the Scenes*:

When the economy started to pick up toward the end of 1980, we were searching for any development that we could showcase to reflect a good trend. [Instead of making the announcement in the pressroom] I had the president fly to Fort Worth [the city with the most dramatic increase in housing starts in the United States], and he made the announcement at a housing development there, surrounded by a bunch of construction workers in hard hats. You get only forty to eighty seconds on any given night on the network news, and unless you can find a visual that explains your message you can't make it stick. [Deaver, 1987:141]

Here is another example of the White House clever manipulation of the medium to convey different messages to different audiences.

When we were going to make an announcement about the placing of a major order for the B-1 bomber, in the early stages of the 1984 campaign, some people close to the president were paranoid over the prospect that Walter Mondale might use this to raise the war and peace issue. But the B-1 bomber had another potential: It meant forty thousand jobs in California. So the decision was made. I wanted the president to be photographed standing next to a B-1 bomber, and I wanted a sign so big that you could barely see the aircraft [on television]. The sign said: Prepared for Peace.... If you can't give me a good visual, give me a big sign. [Deaver, 1987:141]

The White House also knew that the networks craved interesting coverage that evoked an emotional response from viewers. These are referred to as *moments*. Understanding this, media aide Michael Deaver orchestrated stirring moments that television found irresistible. Shortly after the *Challenger* disaster, for example, Reagan gave a superbly crafted speech before a group of schoolchildren in the National Aeronautics and Space Museum in Washington. TV cameras captured the students' facial expressions as the president, flanked by the *Spirit of St. Louis* and the first Apollo moon rocket, lauded the accomplishments of the deceased astronauts. Such a speech would not have had the same impact if it had been delivered in the Rose Garden. On another occasion, the president also gave a speech from the Demilitarized Zone on the border between North and South Korea: "Standing there, staring across that buffer zone, drawing the contrast between freedom and oppression, this was what Ronald Reagan did best" (Deaver, 1987:175).

A high point was reached when the president visited the beaches of Normandy and read a letter from a woman whose father, a veteran of the invasion, had intended to return but had died of cancer. She had vowed to make the pilgrimage for him.

I called the letter to the president's attention, and he took it with him to Normandy and then read it to two thousand visitors [and millions of viewers] at the Omaha Beach memorial, while Lisa Zanatta Henn stood near him: [Reagan said:] "I'm going there, Dad," she had written, "and I'll see the beaches and the barricades and the monuments." As he read, the president's voice began to crack. "I'll see the graves and I'll put flowers there just like you wanted to do. I'll never forget what you went through,

Dad, nor will I let anyone else forget. And, Dad, I'll always be proud." The president's eyes brimmed and he had to choke out the final words. Lisa Henn wept openly. [Deaver, 1987:175–76]

These press tactics were all employed to varying degrees by other presidents. But never were they implemented as thoroughly and as effectively as in the Reagan administration. Through its skillful manipulation of the media, the White House was able to capture and keep the nation's attention on the president's legislative agenda. This resulted in the passage of three of Reagan's top legislative goals during his first year: Congress cut income tax rates by 25 percent, it cut the growth rate of spending on many social service and entitlement programs, and it implemented an unprecedented military buildup. Despite his controversial policies, Reagan, after an initial drop, regained popular approval and was reelected by a wide margin, a feat his televised predecessors found elusive.[2] After a string of aborted and failed presidencies, many analysts felt that Reagan's greatest accomplishment was that he made the presidency work again.

The press strategies that allowed Reagan to overcome extensive-negative coverage contributed to his first-term success but led to disaster during the second. Let us consider how the administration's obsession with secrecy and manipulation of the media nearly led to its political downfall.

THE HIGH PRICE OF SECRECY

The Iran-Contra affair resulted from two important foreign policy objectives of the Reagan administration. The first objective was to free the American and other nationals held hostage in Lebanon. The second was to assist the Nicaraguan Contras in their efforts to topple the Sandinista government.

The Sandinista government took power following a prolonged struggle against Anastasio Somoza, whose family had held power in Nicaragua for 43 years. Concerned that the Left-leaning Sandinista's success would lead to revolutionary activity in neighboring countries (e.g., in El Salvador) as well as give the Soviet Union undue influence in the region, the White House asked for and received congressional funding for the Contras. The American public, however, did not support U.S. involvement in Nicaragua, and on October 12, 1984, Congress cut off all assistance to the Contras.

The president, however, was passionately committed to the Nicaraguan resistance and ordered his staff to find a way to keep the Contras' "body and soul together." To this end, National Security Council staff member Lt. Col. Oliver North formed the "Enterprise." The Enterprise was, in North's words, a "stand alone, off the shelf" organization that the president could turn to for covert activities around the world. Without congressional approval or knowledge, the Enterprise purchased airplanes, airfields, a ship, and communications equipment; hired operatives and public relations firms (to promote the president's Central American policies); and raised millions of dollars from private citizens and other governments (and later from arms sales to Iran), which it stored in secret Swiss bank accounts. These funds were used to aid the Contras despite the congressional ban and despite repeated assurances to the press and the Congress by the president and his staff that they were not.

In 1985 the Israeli government proposed to the Enterprise that missiles be sold to Iran in return for the release of seven U.S. hostages who were being held in Lebanon. The sale meshed well with the president and the Enterprise's interests. If successful, the hostages would be freed and relations with Iran would be improved. The sale would also generate hugh cash reserves that could be used to help the Contras. After several shipments of missiles were completed, however, the total number of hostages held did not decline (some were released, but others were taken), relations between the United States and Iran did not improve, and only $16 million of the $48 million collected by the Enterprise made its way to the Contras. The initiative, however, did generate millions of dollars in commissions for Enterprise operatives. It also violated the U.S. arms embargo against Iran, Congress's ban on aid to the Contras, and the requirement of Section 501 of the National Security Act that Congress be notified in a timely fashion of all significant covert actions undertaken by the United States.

The Iran-Contra scandal dealt a crippling blow to the Reagan administration. Reagan's image as a powerful leader was eroded. Key aides, including the chief of staff, were forced to resign. One attempted suicide. It alienated members of Congress and key segments of the bureaucracy, whose support the president needed in his second term. The revelations also undercut trust and faith in the administration by our allies who were urged by the government not to sell arms to Iran. Some analysts felt it marked the beginning of the end of the Reagan era.

Isolation

What went wrong? A special review panel commissioned by the president concluded that the president had become dangerously isolated from the disastrous impact of his policies and the activities of the unelected and unaccountable National Security Council (NSC) aide who was exercising vast amounts of power on his behalf.

> The President appears to have proceeded with a concept of the initiative that was not accurately reflected in the reality of the operation. The President did not seem to be aware of the way in which the operation was implemented and the full consequences of U.S. participation. . . . He did not force his policy to undergo the most critical review of which the National Security Council participants and the process were capable. At no time did he insist upon accountability and performance review. [*The Tower Commission Report*, 1987:xviii]

Analysts have long noted the tendency for presidents to become isolated (Reedy 1970). Advisers are often intimidated by the office and are reluctant to tell the president when he is making a mistake. Aides hesitate to disagree with an emerging group consensus because they want to be perceived as "team players."

> The principal subordinates to the President must not be deterred from urging the President not to proceed on a highly questionable course of action even in the face of his strong conviction to the contrary. . . . None of them did. All had the opportunity. [*The Tower Commission Report*, 1987:80]

In the Reagan presidency, the problem of isolation was exacerbated by the departure of Jim Baker, Edwin Meese, and Michael Deaver (the famous "troika"). These aides had known the president well. Deaver and Meese had been with President Reagan since his days as governor of California. They complemented his strengths and compensated for his weaknesses. Most of all, they were not reluctant to challenge Reagan when they felt he was wrong. By the second term, however, Deaver had left the White House to become a Washington lobbyist and Meese was appointed attorney general. Jim Baker became Secretary of the Treasury. Their replacements, according to former communications director David Gergen, treated Reagan like "a sort of living national treasure" rather than confronting him when they felt he was in error (Wald, 1987). This was particularly true after the president's landslide win.

The tendency toward isolation was aggravated by the president's leadership style. "The president's management style is to put the principal responsibility for policy review and implementation on the shoulders of his advisors," said *The Tower Commission Report* (1987:79).

The excessive deference inherent in the office of the presidency, the turnover in staff, and the president's management style all contributed to the isolation of the president from the disastrous political consequences of his policies.

Excludes the Press

No claim is made here that the decision to sell arms to Iran and divert profits from those sales to the Contras was a direct result of the president's media policies. Presidents have authorized covert activities of one kind or another long before the advent of television news. Nevertheless, the Iran-Contra scandal suggests that presidents often pay a high price for secrecy: The retreat from reality exhibited by the president and his aides was hastened by the fact that the groups that could have prevented this policy from becoming an enormous scandal—Congress, the foreign policy bureaucracy, and the press—were systematically deceived and manipulated by the president and those around him. The president's leadership style, which included a closed media posture, had created an environment that encouraged such intrigues. Aides boasted about Reagan's political popularity and the White House's skill for manipulating public opinion. Their overconfidence, however, caused them to seriously overestimate their ability to keep this big operation secret and to underestimate the harm their actions, if disclosed, would cause.

The NSC staff used a variety of tactics to dupe the press and the American people. North and John Poindexter repeatedly lied to reporters and congressional committees who queried them about their activities. Trusted aides and political advisers who were close to the president were cut out of the loop because they objected. The president's chief of staff and secretaries of state, defense, and the treasury (who was also a member of the NSC) were not informed because North and Poindexter thought they would leak. Even the director of the CIA, supposedly in charge of covert activities, was apparently not fully informed. North also circumvented the established intelligence bureaucracy, which is a source of news for reporters who cover Washington, by "recruiting former CIA and Defense Department officials, international arms merchants, anti-Castro Cuban terrorists, and soldiers of fortune" (Sharpe, 1987:20). Because the policy was never debated, there were no policy "losers" and therefore no one had an incentive to talk with reporters. The NSC's obsession with secrecy cut the president off from the experts and political advisers who would have alerted him to the detrimental consequences of these activities (Cannon, 1987).

Nevertheless, despite the administration's obsession with secrecy, there is a sense among many journalists that the press was lax (Pear, 1987; Hertsgaard, 1988). Several reasons are cited as to why the press missed the Iran-Contra story. The story was big, complex, and taxed the resources of even the largest news organizations. The press was also reluctant to endanger the lives of the hostages, one of whom—Terry Anderson—was a reporter for the Associated Press. North also charmed and manipulated reporters and publishers and swapped inside information on certain stories in return for promises to keep the lid on others.

In addition, reporters were reluctant to write negative pieces about a president when their criticisms seemed to have no discernible impact on public opinion. Reporters had become weary of writing about "uncounted stupidities, blunders and illegalities with nobody giving a hoot," said *New York Times* reporter Joel Brinkley (M. Stein, 1987:10). The media was also sensitive to a possible backlash from the public if they confronted a popular president on a national security issue (Alter, 1986).

In short, the White House, during the second Reagan administration, had "tamed" the watchdog. By excluding the press from the policy process, however, the president removed an important check from the decision process. Had Reagan been made aware of the foolishness of the initiative, and the misguided nature of the activities that were being undertaken by others on his behalf, but presumably without his knowledge, the uproar from Congress and the public would have forced the president to change course.

CONCLUSION

Ronald Reagan and his staff understood the six o'clock presidency and responded accordingly. Their efforts were specifically tailored to the network news programs because they believed that television was the most important medium covering the president. To cope with extensive coverage, they took fewer questions, held fewer press conferences, kept reporters at a greater distance from the president, and cut them out completely when they felt the need. To deal with negative coverage, they exerted greater control over reporters, restyled the press conference, disposed of cabinet members who became too "hot" after taking the political heat for the president on controversial issues, injected "happy news," and stemmed the flow of government information to the press and the public. Visuals were cleverly used to counteract what emboldened reporters said about the president, his policies, and his staff. To cope with the four seasons, they dominated the news agenda with tactics such as the line of the day and the theme of the week.

In short, the Reagan people captured the medium that had toppled their predecessors. Television news requires simplicity, brevity, personality, and handsome pictures. And the Reagan administration responded with a sound-bite presidency—a simplified, abbreviated, visually oriented, personalized, and thematic chief executive. Because television emphasizes appearance and impressions, sometimes referred to as moments, photo opportunities and elaborately staged media events replaced press conferences. Because television is so dependent on presidential news, the White House fed the networks visually interesting but often content-free pictures, or pictures that even contradicted the administration's policies, with the assurance that they would be given far more prominence on television than they would in print. Although these actions are a rational and predictable response by the White House to the media environment they encountered, these same tactics can have devastating consequences for the nation and the incumbent.

NOTES

1. This statement, displayed on Press Secretary Larry Speakes' desk, caught my eye during a 1986 visit.

2. The fact that Reagan was successful despite the amount of negative coverage (as defined in this study) he received (Chapter 4) suggests that the upbeat visuals that Michael Deaver masterminded seem to have had greater impact on public opinion than the critical copy that correspondents continued to file. In short, what television shows is far more important than what correspondents say. As Sam Donaldson said to me, "A simple truism about television: The eye predominates over the ear when there is a fundamental clash between the two."

9

Alternatives

The previous chapters have presented the thesis that the judgments and needs of television news contribute to the decline—and sometimes the fall—of modern presidents. The extensiveness of television's commitment to coverage of the president and the factors that contribute to a negative portrayal of the incumbent produce a four-staged pattern of reporting themes that, left unchecked, will arise in each televised administration.

The networks build the president up to exalted heights with their initial reporting. Then they bring him down because there is simply nowhere else to go. Their commitment to news coverage of the president, coupled with the need for the news to be novel and entertaining, necessarily leads to finding fault in each administration.

Presidents have responded to the six o'clock presidency by placing greater controls on reporters, by increasing news management efforts, and by cutting access to the president and the flow of information from the executive branch. As we have seen, this can increase the isolation inherent in the office and lead to policy mistakes that harm the nation as well as the president.

Having discussed the impact of the six o'clock presidency on the Reagan and Carter administrations, this chapter's focus is the Bush administration and the patterns likely to characterize presidential-press relations as we move into the next century. We will conclude by considering possibilities for reform.

THE BUSH ADMINISTRATION'S RESPONSE

Early reports suggest that the Bush presidency will be an open administration. Bush has been far more spontaneous and accessible and far less stage-managed than Reagan. During the first 11 months in office, he held 28 more press conferences than Reagan did during his first term in office. Unlike Reagan, who hated uncontrolled encounters with the press, Bush meets with reporters on a moment's notice and chats about a wide variety of subjects. The Bush presidency appears to have no strategic plan (e.g., the line of the day, the theme of the week) for dominating television news.

This very openness, however, makes the new president particularly vulnerable to the six o'clock presidency. Because the White House is not imposing its governing agenda on television, the networks will impose their commercially based agenda on the White House. Reporters will tire of profiling the president, his wife, and his staff. After an initial deluge of positive coverage, attention should shift to the president's legislative agenda. In stark contrast to Reagan, however, Bush does not have a well-defined legislative wish list for Congress. With an unfocused legislative program to cover, the networks will focus on policy flaps and blunders, particularly since care has not been given to the proper packaging of the president's activities for network consumption (Rosenstiel and Gerstenzang, 1989:28). For example, on February 9, 1989, the president gave a major budget speech. The following day, instead of reinforcing his budget themes, he left for Canada to meet with officials about trade and acid rain. Instead of focusing on Bush's speech, and his interpretation of the economy, the networks focused on bad economic news and its *impact* on the new administration (Grove, 1989).

Bush's strategy for dealing with the press by wooing reporters is a throwback to the pretelevised days of Franklin Roosevelt and Harry Truman (Rosenstiel, 1989). Such efforts are a necessary but not sufficient element of a successful press strategy in the age of the electronic presidency. For these reasons, George Bush's coverage will resemble Jimmy Carter's more than Ronald Reagan's.

Furthermore, efforts by Bush aides to ward off negative coverage with Reaganesque press tactics are unlikely to be successful. These tactics require an early start and a consummate performer. And in this regard George Bush is no Ronald Reagan. The president does not have Reagan's charismatic appeal, sense of timing, and other theatrical skills that made Reagan so ideally suited to the televised presidency. (Few politicians do.) In fact, Bush is considered a poor public speaker. In addition, Bush comes to the presidency in the wake of the Iran-Contra scandal, when many Washington insiders and journalists are calling for a more assertive press. Media analysts and journalists have chastised the press for being a poor watchdog for democracy during the Reagan administration (Hertsgaard, 1988).

The new president will also face a new cohort of ambitious correspondents—all of whom will presumably be trying to make a name for themselves—and three news divisions who are engaged in a fierce battle for a shrinking number of viewers. Extensive negative coverage of the presidency is a time-tested programming formula for national fame, network profit, and reduced costs. The thesis suggests that a premature assessment of the president's performance will follow the legislative agenda session. (Soon after, the doors will begin to shut on reporters covering this administration.) Such coverage was foreshadowed on March 7, 1989, six and a half weeks into the new president's term, when CBS aired the following story by Leslie Stahl:

Stahl: The president denied that the Tower fight is diverting his attention from other issues, or that his presidency is floundering.

Bush: It is not adrift, and there isn't malaise.

Stahl: His answer to the growing criticism? Ticking off a list of problems that he has tackled, everything from the savings and loan bailout to his yet-to-be-proposed program for child care.

Bush: I would simply resist the clamor that nothing seems to be bubbling around, that nothing is happening. A lot is happening. Not all of it good. But a lot is happening. . . .

Stahl: Nearly every time President Bush holds a news conference he feels compelled to comment on the state of his inner calmness. Today, again he said that "I still feel relaxed," insisting that the negative reviews of his first 39 days in office haven't rattled him.

THE LONG-TERM RESPONSE

Regardless of the Bush administration's response, the long-term pattern of presidential press relations in the age of television suggests an important irony: Despite the increased effort by the most powerful communications medium available to man, access to the president will continue to decline. It seems inevitable that some future White House will move all or part of the press corps out of the pressroom in the White House to larger quarters, say, in the Executive Office Building. The rationale will be that the press corps has grown too large, but the underlying goal will be to minimize uncontrolled contact between the president and reporters. This may actually result in increased volatility between the presidency and the press, as well as within the press itself, over the issue of press access (the rift between television and print has flared on several occasions). The increased distance between the press and the president will make it impossible for the press to do their jobs effectively, as that job is currently defined.

Future administrations may also try to bypass the White House press completely with the use of controlled media, by, for example, using paid advertisements during the course of the president's term on a regular basis to generate public support for the president and his policies. The development of a weekly White House television show, to replace or complement weekly radio broadcasts, is another way that the president could counterbalance the image of his administration that appears on the evening news.

DETERIORATION OF THE PRESIDENTIAL PRESS CONFERENCE

The widening gulf between the president and the press is particularly evident in the deterioration of the presidential press conference. Presidents are holding fewer and fewer press conferences, and the ones that are held are excoriated by media analysts, working journalists, and White House officials. David Gergen, a former adviser to President Reagan, argues that presidential press conferences do "not serve anyone's purpose very well. They are theater for both sides; the press asks predictable questions and the president gives predictable answers."[1] Three commissions have been set up over the past 14 years to study the presidential press conference. All have concluded that the press conference is in a "distressing state of disrepair" and "not aging well" (Wolfson, 1975; White Burkett Miller Center of Public Affairs, 1981; Kalb and Mayer, 1988).

The dissatisfaction with the press conference sounds like a joke told by comedian and film director Woody Allen. Two elderly Jewish women are having dinner in an upstate New York hotel. One turns to the other and says, "This food is terrible." The other replies, "Yes, and such small portions!"

Likewise, critics complain that modern press conferences are superficial, self-serving, stage-managed spectacles in which no meaningful exchange takes place. Reagan recited well-rehearsed answers to anticipated questions from a preselected list of reporters. Correspondents primp for the cameras. Questions are written in advance and well rehearsed to avoid career-damaging gaffes. Everyone knows that those parts of the conference in which the president trips up will be spot-lighted on the next evening news broadcast.

However, the most frequently cited problem with presidential press conferences is that presidents do not hold enough of them. A recent report by Harvard's Joan Shorenstein Barone Center recommended that the president hold at least 30 press conferences a year. Ronald Reagan's yearly average was six.[2] Such recommendations are unlikely to be implemented because presidents are not obligated by the Constitution to meet with the press (presidents have only been holding press conferences since Teddy Roosevelt's administration, and William H. Taft refused to hold any at all).

The irony spoken of earlier—the fact that the increased efforts by the media have resulted in less, not more, access to the president—is reflected in Figure 9.1. The increased effort by the press is reflected in the growth in the size of the corps, as measured in terms of the number of people who hold official White House press credentials. Figure 9.1 shows that as the corps has grown in size, the frequency of presidential press conferences has declined.[3]

Correlation of course is not causation, but the increase in the number of press credentials reflects the increased commercial viability of the presidency. Presidential news is a growth industry. Moreover, the number of personnel assigned to the White House will continue to climb as mini-cameras and satellite coverage become more available to local TV stations and to foreign news organizations. Thus, if current trends continue, this will mean a continual decline in press conferences. As the media environment has become more formidable, presidents have retreated from the corps.

WHY ACCESS MATTERS

The deterioration of the presidential press conference and the long-term decline in access should concern democracy's friends. French (1982:29–35) argues that the presidential press conference is a unique device that has endured because it serves many important purposes. Her analysis also holds for other occasions where reporters have face-to-face encounters with the president. In the pretelevised presidency, regular meetings with the press provided the president with a forum to educate, inform, and persuade the public through their representatives in the press. The televised press conference, however, is a public relations bonanza for the glib showman, but it tends to severely penalize the less glamorous, but often more thoughtful, statesman.

Access also allows reporters to hold the president accountable for

Figure 9.1
Swelling of White House Press Corps and Decline in Presidential Press Conferences

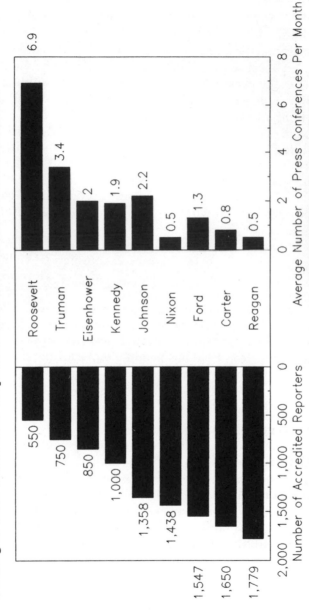

Sources: Number of press conferences from Samuel Kernell, Going Public: New Strategies of Presidential Leadership. Washington, D.C.: Congressional Quarterly Press, 1986, p. 69. The figures for the number of accredited reporters are from several sources. The figure for 1949 is from Cabell Phillips, and others, editor, Dateline: Washington. New York: Doubleday, 1949, p. 148, caption to picture. The figure for 1961 comes from James E. Pollard Presidents and the Press. Truman through Johnson, Washington, D.C.: Public Affairs Press, 1949, p. 97. Figures for 1969 through 1984 were provided by the Secret Service, Department of Public Affairs. 1969 is the first year for which records are available.

his policies, his previous statements, and the behavior of his subordi-
nates. During such exchanges, as was argued earlier, reporters help
keep the president in touch with the world outside the White House.
This cuts down on the built-in tendency for the president to become
isolated. Also, face-to-face encounters give reporters the opportunity to
solicit from the president information his administration may not otherwise serve up. Such information is often critical for an informed assessment of the administration. Reporters also tend to be knowledgeable critics who have an incentive to ask tough questions. Such
exchanges can provide an important check on the presidency, by giving viewers the opportunity to judge the president's character and his
ability to cope with the adverse psychological demands of the job
(Buchanan, 1978).

WHAT CAN BE DONE?

Solutions to the problems caused by the six o'clock presidency fall
into two camps: those that eliminate the source of the injurious pattern
of news coverage of the president and those that control its effects.
Four possible reforms are presented below. The first two reforms address extensive negative coverage, which is the root cause of the six
o'clock presidency. The second two reforms suggest ways to reduce the
six o'clock presidency's effects. (See Table 9.1).

Reform Option 1: Reduce Coverage of the President

The cycle of news coverage of the president described in this book is
partly a function of the scope of the networks' commitment to news
coverage of the president. Thus, covering the president less, according
to the logic of the argument, would defuse the impact of the negative
nature of presidential news. This reform would involve major changes
in network policies concerning the reliance on the White House as a
staple in their broadcasts. Covering the president less would involve
some hardheaded thinking by the networks about the consequences of
their coverage of the president and the examination of some firmly entrenched assumptions about the inherent news value of the president.
(Does he really warrant that much coverage?) Thus, it may be necessary to reassign, or assign on a temporary basis, one or both of the network news crews permanently stationed at the White House and
instead rely more on network pools. This would undercut the incentive
to use White House news. White House reporters would not push for
airtime (a minimum level of which is guaranteed to some in their con-

Table 9.1
Reform Options

Option	Extensive Coverage	Negative Coverage	"Four Seasons"	Access
Reduce Coverage	Less Coverage	No Impact	Mitigate	Possibly Stabilize
Deemphasize Profit	No Impact	Less Negative	Mitigate	Possibly Stabilize
Elect Better Presidents	No Impact	No Impact	Offset	No Impact
Reeducate the Public	Less Coverage	Less Negative	Nullify	Possibly Increase

tracts with the network); the network would not be collecting news it did not use. If the resources were redirected to other areas (e.g., coverage of the regulatory agencies, special-interest groups, the bureaucracy, state government, the Court), the incentive would be further reduced because stories from other sources would be available.

In addition, the networks need to be more selective in their coverage of the presidency. Despite their enormous efforts, 25 years of evening news programming have not improved the quality of the standards citizens use to judge the president. Research suggests that the standards citizens use for judging the president are incomplete, unreasonable, and contradictory (Buchanan, 1987). True, many Americans do not pay as much attention to politics as democratic theorists think they ought to. But it is also the case that one could watch the evening news each night and still be uninformed. David Altheide (1981b) calls this "informed ignorance." Informed ignorance results when citizens are exposed to daily bits and pieces of information that have no political or historical context. Others become psychologically numbed when overloaded with information that they are unable to process. TV news gatekeepers must redefine presidential "news" by asking not "What news will sell?" but "What news do citizens need?" Television news needs to provide citizens the information required to make the kinds of decisions our political system requires them to make, such as assessing presidential performance and choosing among competing candidates for office.

News coverage of the president would still have a negative bias. But without extensive coverage, according to the argument presented here, the four seasons of presidential news would not arise. If the media environment were less formidable, a more open relationship with the press would be less risky for the president.

Reform Option 2: Deemphasize Profit

A second reform addresses the way presidential news is gathered, produced, and reported. For example, if the format of the evening news program were changed (lengthened, with longer reports), reporters could be given more lead time for the preparation of reports and more time in the program in which to air them. News stories about the president could be longer and more complex, detailing the nuances and subtleties that get lost when reports are limited to less than two minutes of airtime. This course of action would also involve a redefinition of news and the altering of assumptions about the nature of the viewing audience (thus reducing the need for conflict, drama, simplicity, pictures, and personalities). Consistent with this series of reforms would be the recruitment of White House reporters with more formal training in history, political science, and economics, who were regarded more for their excellence as journalists rather than their appeal as celebrities.

This reform alternative encompasses a range of options. On one extreme, the networks would simply abandon their pursuit of ratings and profit and offer the evening news programs to the American people as a public service—in exchange for their right to use the nation's airwaves to earn hundreds of millions of dollars in profit each year. Theoretically, this would free news personnel to provide a more erudite news program.

Although this proposal provides an effective cure to the problems caused by the six o'clock presidency, it is unrealistic and impractical. It is also somewhat elitist: It implies that viewers are *solely* interested in trivial and superficial coverage and that viewer preferences should not influence programming decisions. Moreover, if the news programs were, in effect, decommercialized, advertising revenue that permits the networks to cover important events—extended coverage of elections, conventions, and international news—would not be available.

Finally, people are not required to watch the evening news. The most popular noncommercial nationally broadcast news program, PBS'

"MacNeil/Lehrer Newshour," is devoid of many of the problems associated with commercial news broadcasts. But it reaches only a fraction of the viewers that tune into the network news broadcasts. The most learned news program will not inform the mass electorate if only a few people watch.

A more moderate approach would be to deemphasize profits. For the bulk of its existence, CBS's news division was not expected to earn a profit but was subsidized by the huge profits earned by the rest of the corporation (Joyce, 1988). If the three networks were to deemphasize profits for their news divisions, the problems associated with extensive negative coverage would be mitigated. Citizen preferences and affiliate needs would still weigh heavily in news programming decisions, but news executives would have somewhat more flexibility in decisions concerning news coverage of U.S. politics. They would at least have the opportunity to provide more original and innovative coverage. The president would probably still be covered extensively, but the need to be titillating and confrontational would be lessened. For example, there would be more tolerance of "talking heads" such as commentators like Eric Sevaried, who, without snazzy pictures, attempted to put the day's events into a historical and political perspective.

Such reforms, of course, are not likely to be adopted. The networks cover the president the way they do because such coverage satisfies deeply entrenched needs. Without substantial outside force (changes in public viewing habits, competition from local broadcasters, congressional legislation, or regulatory reform), it is unlikely that the networks are going to voluntarily put profits and other concerns aside, especially when they remain convinced that their coverage serves the national interest.

Since reforms that will eliminate the causes of the six o'clock presidency are unlikely to be adopted, let us consider options that attempt to control its effects.

Reform Option 3: Elect More Media-Savvy Presidents

The most frequently suggested reform to the problems of the presidency is to elect "better" presidents. Given the analysis presented here, this would mean electing unusually charismatic presidents who are especially skilled at handling television. An unusually charismatic and telegenic president could, through his use of controlled television, counteract his portrayal in the evening news programs—yet remain open to reporters' queries and criticisms.

There are two major problems with this proposed solution. First, history has shown that while most presidents have been personable, true charismatics are few and far between. For every Roosevelt, Kennedy, and Reagan, there are many more Eisenhowers, Johnsons, Nixons, Fords, Carters, and Bushes—the types of people who are not charismatic enough to counteract the media environment of the modern presidency. Even Ronald Reagan, the consummate showman and television personality, still had to exert substantial control over the way his administration was portrayed by the media.

The second problem with this proposal is that the emphasis on television skills further reduces the presidential talent pool. The American people expect their presidents to look and act the part. Nevertheless, the pretelevised presidency was more tolerant of the disparity between how presidents actually look and sound and our culture's idealized notion of how they *ought* to look and sound. Because television's pictures place so much more emphasis on presidential style than print, it is likely that some of this century's greatest presidents—for example, Theodore Roosevelt, Woodrow Wilson, and Franklin Roosevelt—may not have been elected or perhaps would not have performed as well in office if the evening news covered their campaigns and presidencies. Theodore Roosevelt was too "hot," and his movements too jerky, for a medium that requires "coolness." And Woodrow Wilson would have had great difficulty communicating in sound bites. Viewers would have been reminded each night that their president was crippled if the evening news had covered the Roosevelt administration.[4] Those presidents who have other qualities the presidency requires—energy, intellect, and compassion, for example—but who are merely good on television would be excluded from the nation's highest office. As it is, the campaign season is already too preoccupied with presidential style at the expense of substance. Such a reform would reinforce this already harmful aspect of our electoral process.

Reform Option 4: Reeducate the Public

The final reform option is to encourage citizens to develop better viewing habits. If viewers demand, through their viewing habits, more sophisticated coverage of U.S. politics, the networks will change their coverage accordingly. How do we begin such a monumental task? One place to start is by educating people about television's needs and the way in which those needs shape television's coverage of the presidency and U.S. politics in general. Citizens should be cautious and hard-headed in their evaluation of the president but also of the medium that provides them with information about presidential activities and policies. On a more fundamental level, citizens need to develop more realistic standards for assessing presidential performance. For example, despite television's portrayal, the presidency is not endowed with virtually unlimited power. (There are no buttons to push or levers to pull in order to make the economy run as people think it should!)

The constraints that inhibit presidential action are formidable, and citizens need to be made aware of them. Likewise, if citizens had a greater appreciation for the power of Congress, interest groups, and the bureaucracy, there would be less incentive for the networks to focus as much attention as they do on the affairs of the presidency at six o'clock each evening.

NOTES

1. Speakes, Gergens, and NBC News report quotations about the state of the press conference were taken from Marvin Kalb and Frederick Mayer (1988:10).

2. The Harvard report recommended that the president "should meet with the press on a regularly scheduled basis, twice a month, during daytime hours. In addition to the daytime news conferences, the President should hold a minimum of six televised news conferences a year during evening hours" (Kalb and Mayer, 1988:8–9).

3. Of course, far more people hold credentials than actually cover the president on a daily basis. The official figures allow comparisons to be made across time. Official figures were acquired from the Secret Service and other sources for the following years: 1949, 550; 1961, 1,000; 1969, 1,358; 1972, 1,438; 1973, 1,495; 1975, 1,547; 1977, 1,605; 1978, 1,642; 1980, 1,664; 1984, 1,696; 1986, 1,779. The figure for 1949 come from Phillips et al., (1949:148, caption to picture). The figure for 1961 comes from Pollard (1964:97). Figures for 1969 through 1984 were provided by the Secret Service, Department of Public Affairs; 1969 is the first year that records are available from the Secret Service.

4. Newspapers did not print pictures of Franklin Roosevelt when he was using his wheelchair.

Appendix A

Examples of Positive, Neutral, and Negative Stories

POSITIVE STORY

Rather: What a difference a day makes. A day after his public complaint to President Reagan about getting a red-tape runaround, artificial heart recipient William Schroeder today got his Social Security disability check, hand-delivered to his bedside. Bruce Morton reports on what it takes to quicken the pulse of the bureaucracy.

Woman (in Social Security office): Yes, I get these next Tuesday.

Man (Social Security office clerk): Several weeks of processing, I would think 'cause—

Bruce Morton: That's life in Social Security's slow lane, where most people live. Not artificial heart recipient William Schroeder, who used a phone call from the president yesterday to put bureaucracy into high gear.

William Schroeder (on telephone yesterday): Just keep on calling and keep on calling and I don't get anywhere.

Voice of President Ronald Reagan (over phone): Bill, I will get into it and find out what this situation is.

Morton: Schroeder's tactics drew applause from his friends (applause, laughter). And the president did get into it. Boy, did he get into it! The check traveled to Louisville by jet, nestled in bureaucratic arms.

Man (presenting check): The president took a great deal of interest in your case, contacted Social Security. We're sorry for the delays in your case, and we're here to present you with the check for benefits that you had due today.

Schroeder: Oh, thank you very much.

Man: Thank you.

Schroeder: Well, you want to feel my heart?

Morton: The official explanation was, well, we just speeded things up a tiny bit.

Martha McSteen (Social Security commissioner): Perhaps the decision would have been made normally in another two weeks, so we were just able to speed up that process.

Morton: But a Social Security Administration worker in a local office had this reaction to the news that the check arrived in a single day.

Man (Social Security worker): Wow! I think that's amazing!

Morton: And one of the people who'd been waiting in line was glad for Schroeder, but—

Woman: I understand the circumstance that he is in. I just wish that the Social Security Administration might be a little bit helpful towards other people also.

Morton: In fact, Mr. Fix-It is a role the president has played often: a change in Medicare rules so that little Katie Beckett could go home from the hospital; Social Security benefits for Scott Oliveira's mother; a liver transplant donor for Ashley Bailey.

President Reagan (over the telephone): Well, these calls between the two of us are becoming a habit.

Morton: Mr. Reagan likes the phone and he's good at it. One Democratic congressman grumped, "Maybe that's the only way to get the bureaucracy moving." So, problems with the Veterans Administration? With Social Security? Call the nice man at the White House. Operators are standing by to take your call.[1]

NEUTRAL STORY

Anchor: President Carter gave his final approval today to plans for a new generation of nuclear missiles. The MX mobile force would take ten years to build, at a cost of $33 billion. The president said he hoped it

would be "the last missile system of enormous destructive power we will ever have to build." More from Leslie Stahl.

Leslie Stahl: President Carter made the announcement himself, saying the new system is not a bargaining chip to be used in the SALT talks but rather a system that the U.S. needs for its national security, since, he said, the threat to our current missile system is real.

President Jimmy Carter: Deploying this system will make it clear to the Soviet Union that they will gain no strategic advantage out of continuing the nuclear arms race. The system is survivable, it's verifiable, it has a minimum impact on the environment, it's affordable in cost, and it's consistent with our SALT goals of deep reductions in strategic arms.

Leslie Stahl: Under the plan, the U.S. will house 200 MX missiles on government-owned land in the deserts of Utah and Nevada. The system is a pattern of railroad tracks and dirt roads along which the missiles will be transported and then secretly housed in underground shelters. There'll be one missile for each roadway. Once a month in times of peace, a flatbed transporter will change the missile's location by shuttling it along an oval-shaped open road, approaching each of 23 underground shelters and secretly depositing the missile in one of them. In case of attack, the missile can be moved quickly from one shelter to another or could be launched directly. In all, there will be 4,600 shelters, each about a mile apart, so if the Russians wanted to knock out the system, they'd have to deploy thousands of missiles. The main attraction, according to Defense Secretary Harold Brown, is the dash capability, meaning that the missiles can be moved quickly.

Harold Brown (Secretary of Defense): This system is such that the Soviets will have a very difficult time planning to attack it, which is, of course, what deterrence is all about. Even if they know where everyone is when they fire their ICBMs, they won't know where they'll be when their ICBMs arrive.

Stahl: Pentagon officials say the new system will convince the other side that it's not to its advantage to strike first. As one official said, "The real purpose is to keep people from pushing buttons."[2]

NEGATIVE STORY

Anchor: White House Chief of Staff Hamilton Jordan reportedly has hired Watergate prosecutor Henry Ruth to represent him in the investigation of allegations that he once used cocaine. The Associated Press quotes knowledgeable sources as saying Jordan retained Ruth the day after the FBI investigation. The FBI report is expected this

week. Attorney General Civiletti will then have to decide whether this situation warrants appointment of a special prosecutor.[3]

NOTES

1. Bruce Morton, CBS News, Washington, DC, December 13, 1984.
2. Leslie Stahl, CBS News, White House, Washington, DC, September 7, 1979.
3. Walter Cronkite, CBS News, New York, September 4, 1979.

Appendix B

Interviewing the White House Press

In addition to the coding of the "CBS Evening News" transcripts, I spent several weeks with the White House press corps in the pressroom and on the road. As a participant–observer I was able to interview correspondents, editors, network executives for all three networks, and White House officials. This appendix shares additional thoughts about the collection of these data.[1]

PARTICIPANT–OBSERVER

A review of the literature suggested that decisions made at four levels within CBS helped shape the content, tone, and amount of coverage the president received. Accordingly, the first task was to interview individuals at each level and, if possible, observe them in action. The purpose of the interviews was to gain insight into the goals, environmental constraints, and network policies associated with news coverage of the president. I was particularly interested in how press coverage of the president had changed since the introduction of television and how news coverage varies during the course of an individual presidency.

ACCESS TO THE SITE

Entry to the White House pressroom for the initial five-day visit in spring 1982 was easily obtained. About two months prior to my planned arrival, I wrote the press office, requesting permission to visit the pressroom for a few days. Shortly thereafter, I received word from the White House press office that my request had been granted. The purpose of this visit was, in Richard Fenno's (1978) words, to "soak and poke." I had no formal interviews scheduled, but I did speak with several network technicians, journalists, and White House staff. I also attended the afternoon briefing given by Larry Speakes each day and two presidential functions. I watched President Reagan, flanked by congressional leaders, announce that a compromise had been reached on a plan to save Social Security. I also attended a "prayer day" celebration in which the president announced his support for a constitutional amendment to allow prayer in public schools. I observed the network technical crews setting up for each of these events, and I watched the various network correspondents prepare and deliver their stand-ups on the White House lawn. Both events were reported on the evening news. My visit to the White House gave me a visual image of the environment in which White House correspondents work.

During this visit, I spoke with several persons who had been—or who were presently—involved in the gathering, selection, or production of presidential news for CBS, ABC, and NBC.[2]

I quickly realized, however, the presidential press relations were much more complicated than I had anticipated and that a longer visit would be necessary to put these observations into perspective. I had the good fortune to meet ABC's David Brinkley following a presentation he gave in January 1986. Brinkley wrote a letter to Deputy Press Secretary Larry Speakes on my behalf, requesting a longer visit. This request was also approved. During summer 1986, I observed the press at work for two weeks (June 6–20) in the pressroom in the White House. The third week was spent "on the road," first in Las Vegas for a presidential fund-raiser for Senate hopeful Jim Santini in Nevada (June 25) and then in Santa Barbara (June 26–29). I also observed the editing process in ABC's and NBC's Washington bureaus, in addition to speaking with several correspondents, producers, technicians, and White House officials.[3]

EXPLORING THE PHYSICAL SITE

Soon after gaining access to the pressroom, one of my first tasks was to explore the environment in which presidential press relations take place. I began by drawing a map (Figure B.1) of the main pressroom and the upper and lower press offices. This focused my attention on the physical environment in which reporters work. An inspection of the site provided important information and insights that would not have been available had I relied exclusively on interviews. For example, the fact that the original White House architect did not provide space for reporters suggests that the Framers of the Constitution did not anticipate the level and intensity of press coverage the president receives today, which is why the current pressroom sits on top of the White House pool.

The physical conditions in which people labor is an important determinant of how they go about their work and how they feel about their job. This matters because the room in which White House correspondents spend their days and in which they form impressions about the president is unpleasant. The individual booths that each network has in the back of the pressroom (Figure B.1) are not much bigger than walk-in closets. They are cramped and crowded, without windows, and providing little privacy. The poor conditions in the pressroom is one reason why there is such high turnover in network personnel. This has important consequences for news coverage of the president because high turnover results in network correspondents with less expertise and perspective than, for instance, the wire service reporters who have covered several administrations.

The tight quarters also contributes to the homogenization of reporting, known as "pack journalism." For example, after a Reagan presidential press conference that I attended, reporters from the three networks did not depart for their news bureaus scattered throughout Washington. Instead, they chatted outside their booths with one another about the president's performance. Realizing that it was during these informal conversations that correspondents come to important conclusions, which they would soon share with millions of viewers, White House aides moseyed over. They said they were there to answer any questions the press might have about the president's press conference, but the real purpose of the "Spin Patrol," as correspondent Bill Plante of CBS referred to them, was to put the proper "spin" or interpretation on the press conference by highlighting the parts where the president did well and downplaying the parts where he performed poorly.

On further exploration of the site, I discovered a feature indicating the social structure of the press corps. Underneath each of the forty-eight pressroom chairs is a gold plate identifying an assigned news organization. In Washington, proximity to power is an important indicator of importance; where people sit announces their position in an organization. Thus, when you turn the seat bottoms up, as I did one

Figure B.1
Pressroom Seating in West Wing of White House

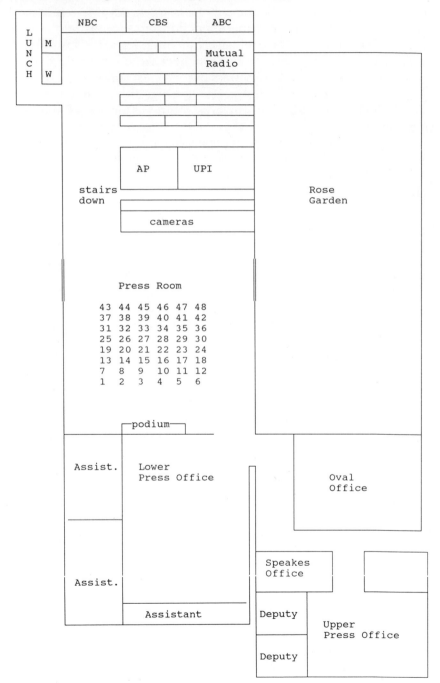

Figure B.1 (continued)

1. Reuter
2. ABC
3. UPI
4. CBS
5. AP
6. NBC
7. AFP
8. Washington Post
9. Detroit News
10. NY Daily News
11. Time
12. Wall Street Journal
13. NY Times
14. United Stations
15. LA Times
16. Newsweek
17. UPI Radio
18. Newsday
19. CNN
20. Chicago Sun Times
21. US News and World Report
22. Knight Ridder
23. Mutual
24. AP Radio

25. Washington Times
26. Gannett
27. Baltimore Sun
28. Boston Globe
29. Voice of America
30. Chicago Tribune
31. Scripps Howard
32. BNA Broadcast News America
33. INN
34. Dallas Times Herald
35. Metromedia
36. NewHouse
37. Cox
38. Dallas Morning News
39. ICA
40. National Public Radio
41. Sheridan
42. McClendon
43. Christian Science Monitor
44. Hearst
45. St. Louis Post Dispatch
46. Blank
47. Westinghouse
48. Trans Features

Where the organizations are placed is due in part to their importance—e.g., the national media are in the front row—and to how long they have been covering the White House.

Sunday afternoon when few people were around, the social stratification or "pecking order" of the White House pressroom is revealed. The fact that the three networks are all seated in the front row (along with the wires), a pattern repeated on the White House press plane (network correspondents are seated in first class), suggests that while all reporters are equal in the eyes of the First Amendment, some reporters are more equal than others in the eyes of the White House.

INTERVIEWING THE CORRESPONDENTS

Correspondents have few incentives and many disincentives to being interviewed. Deadline pressure, competition, interruptions, and a wariness and weariness of academics and other "outsiders" initially inhibited extended and informative conversation. One correspondent declined to be interviewed. Another groused that I was the second academic to interview him this month. He had also received a lengthy questionnaire in the mail. A third said she would speak to me for ten minutes but that she "was not thrilled about doing it." "Another time" was the most typical response. Those that did speak with me expressed concern that their words would come back to haunt them. One well-known, often aggressive correspondent ended the interview by asking me "to be kind" to her in what I wrote. Another interview was interrupted by a bureau chief who reminded the correspondent that I was taping. In addition, a cameraperson I spoke with at length was chastised for her candor by a colleague: "You know, we don't really know who this guy really is," she was told. "He could be a spy from Capitol Cities," the corporation that recently purchased ABC.

These responses are not altogether surprising. Like the powerful political actors they cover, correspondents and the networks that employ them have come under increasing scrutiny by secular and religious interest groups, Washington think tanks, the courts, and academia. They are cautious about to whom they speak and very careful about what they say.

Although not quite rebuffed, I decided to retreat and spend my initial days in the pressroom observing, taking notes, and taking pictures (when other cameramen were snapping away). During this time, I developed a rapport with several technicians. From them I learned many of the unwritten rules that guide the day-to-day interaction between the press and the White House. Eventually, I did get several hours of informative conversation with seven of the ten correspondents.

LEARNING THE ROPES

I got through to the correspondents by "learning the ropes" of the White House pressroom, the ebb and flow of the day's routines, the norms that undergird the fairly complex sets of relationships correspondents have with the Secret Service, the White House, the network, and their crew and among themselves. The Secret Service has established rules about where one can walk, sit, and stand; the White House has rules concerning the use of videotape, sound equipment, and still and flash photography; and reporters have norms concerning competition and cooperation.

Failure to learn the ropes can be embarrassing and costly. For example, one night following a presidential press conference, I almost crossed an invisible infrared beam used to alert the Secret Service of a prowler on the White House lawn. A break in the beam causes an alarm to go off, lights to turn on, and—I suppose—sharpshooters to take aim. Fortunately, a technician called to me in time. On another occasion, I moved (slightly) about on a platform while cameramen were getting critical footage of President Reagan. The movement jostled their tripods and incurred their wrath. (I was soon forgiven.) The point is that the pressroom is littered with "land mines" that the newcomer must avoid. Fenno's (1978: 264) words were especially helpful: "Mostly, of course, the way you establish good rapport is by being nice to people and trying to see the world as they see it. You need to be patient, come on slow, and feel your way along. Two handy hints: Go where you are driven; take what you are given; and, when in doubt, be quiet."

I felt that it was very important to establish the seriousness of my project nonverbally—by hanging around for several weeks; by traveling long distances, at personal expense; and by talking to other reporters, members of the White House staff, and network technicians. An extended stay helped dispel the notion that I was on a "hit and run" mission, looking for good quotes to spice up an article, or from an organization "out to get" the press. The extended stay also meant that I could catch reporters on slow news days, on "off" days when a correspondent was not responsible for that evening's spot, or when a news "lid" was on, meaning that no news would be coming from the White House for a specified period.

THE TECHNICIANS

The cameramen and soundmen for the three networks were critical to the success of this project. Unlike the correspondents, who retreat to their booths, the technicians stay in the main pressroom. There is nowhere else for them to go. The technicians have more free time than the correspondents, are under less pressure, and have more reasonably sized egos. They were also more willing to talk about their work (sometimes in greater technical detail than I cared to hear). They answered many of the questions I was going to put to the correspondents and were a sounding board for others. They were also more candid and forthcoming. This seemed to be due to their naturally irreverent manner and their appreciation for the attention they were receiving from a college professor writing a book about what they did for a living. Finally, the technicians are among the most senior people in the pressroom, having served in the White House many years longer than the correspondents, White House officials, and—with the exception of the wire services—most of the other reporters. They had an institutional memory not shared by the correspondents.

I befriended several from one network, and they introduced me to others. Once the word got around about who I was and what I was up to, this time communicated by others, many technicians began instigating conversations with me, sending others over to talk, and suggesting people with whom I should speak. This activity did not go unnoticed by several of the correspondents, who tend to be very sensitive to changes in the pressroom milieu. Sam Donaldson, ABC, for example, said that I appeared to be a "serious fellow," although I had not spoken with him, and *he invited me* back into his booth to talk. This was my breakthrough.

INTERVIEWING

The interviewing of correspondents differs considerably from the types of interviewing typically done by political scientists of, say, congressmen or voters. This usually involves the preparation of a fairly extensive, carefully worded, and arranged series of questions that are put to a passive respondent during the course of a 45-minute meeting, scheduled several weeks in advance.

Reporters are not receptive to this format. The unpredictable nature of the news business works against their committing to a prearranged meeting. Instead, the interviewer must work at the reporter's convenience, which generally means on a "catch-as-catch-can" basis. Thus, a "45-minute" interview will probably take place 10 to 15 minutes at a time, often over the course of several days—in cars, on planes, or while walking to or from an event.

Second, White House correspondents are anything but passive. Several were aggressive, verbal, hyperactive, type-A individuals. It was not uncommon for them to turn on a "canned" pitch—usually about the

White House's control over reporters' movements and the inaccessibility of President Reagan. Since this was not the main focus of my research, and since my time was very brief, I had to devise ways of cutting through the dross. I generally let the correspondent go on for a minute or two. Then I politely nodded and moved to another question. Other times I would break eye contact; in one case, I changed tapes in my recorder.[4] These are nonverbal cues reporters use to accomplish similar ends during their interviews.

The interview guide I had prepared for the trip was fairly long and involved. Of particular interest to me were reporter goals, the constraints they faced, and the strategies they used for overcoming those constraints. Other questions concerned reporter career paths, "turnover" in the pressroom, and the social structure of the pressroom. As it turned out, I was unable to follow the interview guide in a ticktock, question-after-question fashion. The lengthy interview guide (five single-spaced pages) was a turnoff to the reporters, who saw a time-consuming task ahead. Instead, I developed several short but broadly based questions that I used to structure the conversation. One of these, for example, was: Can you describe a typical day at the White House? This main question would "get the reporter going," and I could interject other questions (e.g., Could you give me an example of that?) as our discussion continued. This semistructured format was much more applicable to the situation I encountered in the White House. What resulted was a series of "informing conversations" rather than formal interviews—each providing a piece of the larger story I was attempting to tell.

By going on the road with the press, I was able to see the press interact with one another and with the general public, as well as to observe the lengths to which the networks will go to get pictures of the president.

The purpose of the participant research was both to explore old questions and to develop new ones. Here is an example of how my visit with the press corps influenced the six o'clock presidency thesis.

While I was interviewing correspondent Sam Donaldson in his hotel suite in Santa Barbara, California, a nearby amusement park pier caught fire. The pier had been badly damaged in a storm and had just recently been rebuilt. Eyeing the large plume of smoke rising from the pier, Donaldson said, "I'm going to cover this. Do you want to come along?" This seemed novel, so I said, "Sure." In a flurry of activity, he summoned sound and camerapersons. With their equipment in tow, we jumped into a rented Cadillac. As we were pulling away, one of the crew noticed that her mini-cam's battery was low. She darted back to her room to get a fresh one—but after harsh words were exchanged with the correspondent.

A crowd of several hundred had gathered by the time we got down to the waterfront. The correspondent jumped out of the car and started running to the pier. As we made our way over barricades and water hoses, someone shouted, "Hey, it's Sam Donaldson." "Go get'em, Sam," the crowd cheered. Even some of the firemen who were involved in battling the blaze turned their heads, and an article in the next day's local paper made mention of the correspondent's presence at the fire.

This experience—the partial upstaging of a fire by a reporter—reemphasized in my mind the celebrity status of the men and women who cover the president for the network news.

NOTES

1. See Lofland and Lofland (1984); Shaffir, Stebbins, Turowetz (1980); Habenstein (1970).

2. At CBS News in New York, I spoke with three CBS News vice presidents, two of whom are involved in the day-to-day gathering and production of news (John Lane, Ernest Leiser). A third, Ralph Goldberg, is a vice president and assistant to the president of CBS News. Goldberg is an attorney and has functioned as an associate general counsel for CBS. At NBC, I spoke with former correspondent and now NBC vice president Tom Pettit and with Richard Salant, who is a past president of CBS News. I also spoke with Bill Small, of United Press International (UPI), who was Washington bureau chief for CBS News during the Nixon administration. In CBS's Washington bureau, I spoke with bureau chief Jack Smith and Susan Zirinski, a producer for the evening news. In ABC's Washington bureau, I spoke with Rex Granum, deputy director of television news, who was an aide to Jody Powell in the Carter administration. At this time, I spoke with Washington correspondents Leslie Stahl (White House), Phil Jones (former White House correspondent; now at Capitol Hill), and Robert Pierpoint, who covered the White House for more than 20 years.

3. I spoke with David Brinkley, Sam Donaldson (ABC); Bill Plante, Leslie Stahl, Gary Schuster (CBS); and Chris Wallace and Andrea Mitchell (NBC). I also spoke with a number of producers and technicians for the three networks, among them David Kaplan, Ginny Vicario, Douglas Almond (all from ABC), and Gene Gerlach of CBS News. I also had the chance to chat with several members of the White House press office, including Acting Press Secretary Larry Speakes and his assistant, Mark Weinberg.

4. All the interviews were tape-recorded on 60-minute cassette tapes. The use of the tape recorder allowed me to maintain eye contact and to jot down questions as they arose. No one objected to its use. To be polite—as well as save tape—I turned the recorder off when conversations were interrupted by phone calls or visitors. These tapes were transcribed onto a personal computer. This allowed convenient access to a complete, verbatim set of the conversations.

References

Abel, Elie, ed. 1981. *What's News.* San Francisco: Institute for Contemporary Studies.

Adams, William, and Philip Heyl. 1981. "From Cairo to Kabul with the Networks, 1972–1980." In *Television Coverage of the Middle East,* ed. William C. Adams, pp. 1–39. Norwood, NJ: Ablex.

Adams, William, and Fay Schreibman, eds. 1978. *Television Network News: Issues in Content Research.* Washington, DC: School of Public and International Affairs.

Agnew, Spiro T. 1972. "Speech Given to the Midwest Regional Republican Committee Meeting in Des Moines, Iowa." In *The Impudent Snobs: Agnew vs. the Intellectual Establishment,* ed. John R. Coyne. New York: Arlington House.

Alpern, David M., and Eleanor Clift. 1983. "President vs. Press." *Newsweek,* February 14, p. 21.

Alter, Jonathan. 1986. "Will There Be a Backlash?" *Newsweek,* December 15, p. 40.

Altheide, David L. 1976. *Creating Reality: How T.V. News Distorts Events.* Beverly Hills, CA: Sage.

Altheide, David L. 1981a. "Iran vs. U.S. TV News: The Hostage Story Out of Context." In *Television Coverage of the Middle East,* ed. William C. Adams, pp. 128–57. Norwood, NJ: Ablex.

Altheide, David L. 1981b. "Network News Oversimplified and Underexplained." *Washington Journalism Review* 3: 28–29.

Altheide, David L. 1985. "Impact of Format and Ideology on TV News Coverage of Iran." *Journalism Quarterly* 62: 346–51.

Altheide, David L., and Robert P. Snow. 1979. *Media Logic*. Beverly Hills, CA: Sage.

Armbister, Trevor. 1971. *A Matter of Accountability: The True Story of the Pueblo Affair*. New York: Coward-McCann.

Bagdikian, Benjamin H. 1971. *The Information Machines: Their Impact on Men and the Media*. New York: Torch Books.

Balutis, Alan P. 1976. "Congress, the President and the Press." *Journalism Quarterly* 53 (Fall): 509–15.

Balutis, Alan P. 1977. "The Presidency and the Press: The Expanding Image." *Presidential Studies Quarterly* 7 (Fall): 251.

Barber, James D. 1980. *The Pulse of Politics: Electing Presidents in the Media Age*. New York: W. W. Norton.

Barger, H. M. 1984. *The Impossible Presidency*. Glenview, IL: Scott Foresman.

Barnouw, Eric. 1970. *The Image Empire: A History of Broadcasting in the United States from 1953*. New York: Oxford University Press.

Barrett, Marvin, ed. 1974. *Moment of Truth*. New York: Harper-Colophon.

Barrett, Marvin. 1978. *Rich News, Poor News*. New York: Crowell.

Batscha, Robert M. 1975. *Foreign Affairs News and the Broadcast Journalist*. New York: Praeger.

Berdes, George. 1969. *The Friendly Adversaries*. Marquette University: Center for the Study of the American Press.

Bethel, Tom. 1977. "The Myth of an Adversary Relationship." *Harper's*, January, pp. 33–40.

Blair, Gwenda. 1988. *Almost Golden*. New York: Simon and Schuster.

Blumenthal, Sidney. 1981. *The Permanent Campaign*. New York: Simon and Schuster.

Bonafede, Dom. 1975. "Nessen Still Seeks 'Separate Peace' with Press." *National Journal*, October 11, p. 1412.

Bonafede, Dom. 1979. "Has the Rafshoon Touch Left Its Mark on the White House?" *National Journal*, April 14, pp. 588–93.

Bonafede, Dom. 1982. "The Washington Press—It Magnifies the President's Flaws and Blemishes." *National Journal*, May 1, pp. 767–71.

Bonafede, Dom. 1986. "Press Focus." *National Journal*, February 22, p. 480.

Boot, William. 1987. "Iranscam: When the Cheering Stopped." *Columbia Journalism Review*, March-April, pp. 25–30.

Boyer, Peter J. 1988. *Who Killed CBS?* New York: Random House.

Boylan, James. 1986. "Declarations of Independence." *Columbia Journalism Review*, November-December, pp. 30–45.

Braestrup, Peter. 1978. *Big Story*. Garden City, NY: Anchor Books.

Brandt, Ed. 1969. *The Last Voyage of the USS Pueblo*. New York: Norton.

Breed, Warren. 1955. "Social Control in the Newsroom: A Functional Analysis." *Social Forces* 33 (May): 326–35.

Broder, David. 1969. "Views of the Press: Political Reporters in Presidential Politics." *Washington Monthly* 1 (February): 33.

Broder, David. 1975. "The Presidency and the Press." In *The Future of the Amer-*

ican Presidency, ed. Charles W. Dunn, pp. 255–68. Morristown, NJ: General Learning Press.

Broder, David. 1987. *Behind the Front Page*. New York: Simon and Schuster.

Brody, Richard A., and Benjamin I. Page. 1975. "The Impact of Events on Presidential Popularity: The Johnson and Nixon Administrations." In *Perspectives on the Presidency*, ed. Aaron Wildavsky, pp. 136–48. Boston: Little, Brown.

Broh, C. Anthony. 1980. "Horse Race Journalism: Reporting the Polls in the 1976 Presidential Election." *Public Opinion Quarterly* 44 (Winter): 514–29.

Brown, Les. 1971. *Television: The Business behind the Box*. New York: Harcourt, Brace, Jovanovich.

Brown, Les. 1979. *Keeping Your Eye on Television*. New York: Pilgrim Press.

Buchanan, Bruce. 1978. *The Presidential Experience*. Englewood Cliffs, NJ: Prentice-Hall.

Buchanan, Bruce. 1987. *The Citizen's Presidency*. Washington, DC: Congressional Quarterly.

Bunce, Richard. 1976. *Television and the Corporate Interest*. New York: Praeger.

"Bushwacked." 1988. *Time*, September 8, pp. 16–20.

Buss, Terry F., and C. Richard Hofstetter. 1977. "The Logic of Television News Coverage of Political Campaign Information." *Journalism Quarterly* 54 (Summer): 341–49.

Cannon, Lou. 1977. *Reporting: An Inside View*. Sacramento: California Journal Press.

Cannon, Lou. 1987. "The High Cost of Secrecy." *Washington Post*, July 20, p. A2.

Carter, Jimmy. 1982. *Keeping Faith*. New York: Bantam.

"Carter Will Avoid Press on Occasion." 1977. *New York Times*, February 6, p. 28.

Cater, Douglass. 1986. "The Anchor Isn't the Story." *New York Times*, March 22, p. 15.

Chancellor, John, and Walter R. Mears. 1983. *The News Business*. New York: Harper & Row.

Christian, George. 1970. *The President Steps Down*. New York: Macmillan.

Cohen, Bernard. 1963. *The Press and Foreign Policy*. Princeton, NJ: Princeton University Press.

Collier, Barney. 1975. *Hope and Fear in Washington*. New York: Dial Press.

Comstock, George. 1980. *Television in America*. Beverly Hills, CA: Sage.

Cornwell, Elmer E. 1965. *Presidential Leadership of Public Opinion*. Bloomington: Indiana University Press.

Cornwell, Elmer E. 1974. *The Presidency and the Press*. Morristown, NJ: General Learning Press.

Cronin, Thomas. 1974. "The Presidency Public Relations Script." In *The Presidency Reappraised*, ed. R. G. Tugwell and Thomas E. Cronin, pp. 168–83. New York: Praeger.

Cronin, Thomas. 1980. *The State of the Presidency*. 2d ed. Boston: Little, Brown.

Crouse, Timothy. 1972. *The Boys on the Bus*. New York: Random House.

Cutler, Lloyd N. 1984. "Foreign Policy on Deadline." *Foreign Policy* 56: 113–28.

Darton, Robert. 1975. "Writing News and Telling Stories." *Daedalus*, Spring, pp. 175–94.

Davidson, Roger, and Glenn R. Parker. 1972. "Positive Support for Political Institutions: The Case of Congress." *Western Political Quarterly* 25 (December): 610.

Deaver, Michael. 1987. *Behind the Scenes*. New York: William Morrow.

Dennis, Everett E., and William L. Rivers. 1974. *Other Voices: The New Journalism in America*. San Francisco: Canfield Press.

de Tocqueville, Alexis. 1969. *Democracy in America*, ed. J. P. Mayer. Garden City: Anchor Books.

Diamond, Edwin. 1977. "President Carter on the Airwaves—Echoes of F.D.R." *New York Times*, March 20, p. 29.

Diamond, Edwin. 1980. *Good News, Bad News*. Cambridge, MA: MIT Press.

Diamond, Edwin. 1981. "Press Watch: Putting Your Best Facts Forward." *Washington Journalism Review*, May, p. 49.

Dickerson, Nancy. 1976. *Among Those Present: A Reporter's View of Twenty-Five Years in Washington*. New York: Random House.

Donaldson, Sam. 1987. *Hold On, Mr. President!* New York: Random House.

Dorman, William A., and Mensour Farhang. 1987. *The U.S. Press and Iran*. Berkeley: University of California Press.

Dorman, William A., and Ehsan Ommed. 1979. "Reporting Iran the Shah's Way." *Columbia Journalism Review*, January-February, pp. 27–33.

D'Souza, Dinesh. 1986. "TV News: The Politics of Social Climbing." *Policy Review* 37 (Summer): 24–31.

Dunn, Deimer D. 1969. *Public Officials and the Press*. Menlow Park, CA: Addison-Wesley.

Edwards III, George C. 1980. *Presidential Influence in Congress*. San Francisco: W. H. Freeman.

Edwards III, George C. 1983. *The Public Presidency: The Pursuit of Popular Support*. New York: St. Martin's Press.

Efron, Edith. 1970. "There Is a Network News Bias." *TV Guide*, February 28, pp. 7–11.

Ellerbee, Linda. 1986. *"And So It Goes."* New York: G. P. Putnam's Sons.

Epstein, Edward. 1973a. *News from Nowhere*. New York: Random House.

Epstein, Edward. 1973b. "The Selection of Reality." *New Yorker*, March 3, pp. 41–64.

Epstein, Edward. 1975. *Between Fact and Fiction: The Problem of Journalism*. New York: Vintage Books.

Fallows, James. 1979. "The President and the Press." *Washington Monthly*, October, pp. 9-17.

Fedler, Fred; Mike Meeske; and Joe Hall. 1979. "Time Magazine Revisited: Presidential Stereotypes Persist." *Journalism Quarterly* 56 (Summer): 353–59.

Feiman, Jeffrey. 1977. *The Newscasters*. New York: Manor Books.

Fenno, Richard F. 1973. *Congressmen in Committees*. Boston: Little, Brown.

Fenno, Richard F. 1978. *Homestyle.* Boston: Little, Brown.

Ford, Gerald. 1979. *A Time to Heal.* New York: Harper & Row.

French, Blaire Atherton. 1982. *The Presidential Press Conference.* Lanhama, MD: University Press of America.

Friendly, Fred W. 1978. *Due to Circumstances beyond Our Control.* New York: Vintage Books.

Gans, Herbert J. 1979. *Deciding What's News: A Study of CBS Evening News, NBC Nightly News, Newsweek, and Time.* New York: Pantheon.

Gates, Gary Paul. 1978. *Airtime: The Inside Story of CBS News.* New York: Berkeley.

Gergen, David. 1982. "Meeting the Press: A Conversation with David Gergen and Jody Powell." *Public Opinion,* December–January.

Germond, Jack W., and Jules Witcover. 1977. "Bert Lance, the Washounds and Dog Days in Washington." *Columbia Journalism Review,* November-December, pp. 27–31.

Gilbert, Robert E. 1972. *Television and Presidential Politics.* North Quincy, MA: Christopher Publishing House.

Gilbert, Robert E. 1981. "Television and Political Power." *Journal of Social, Political and Economic Studies* 6 (Spring): 75–93.

Gitlin, Todd. 1980. *The Whole World Is Watching: Mass Media in the Making and Unmaking of the New Left.* Berkeley: University of California Press.

Glad, Betty. 1980a. *Jimmy Carter and the Great White House.* New York: Norton.

Glad, Betty. 1980b. *Mass Media and American Politics.* Washington, DC: Congressional Quarterly.

Graber, Doris A. 1972. "Personal Qualities in Presidential Images: The Contribution of the Press." *Midwest Journal of Political Science* 16: 46–76.

Greider, William. 1981. *The Education of David Stockman and Other Americans.* New York: Dutton.

Grossman, Michael B., and Martha J. Kumar. 1981. *Portraying the President.* Baltimore: Johns Hopkins University Press.

Grossman, Michael B., and Francis E. Rourke. 1976. "The Media and the Presidency: An Exchange Analysis." *Political Science Quarterly,* Fall, pp. 464–66.

Grove, Lloyd. 1989. "Putting Teflon to the Test." *Washington Post National Weekly Edition,* 2/27–3/5, pp. 13–14.

Habenstein, Robert W. 1970. *Pathways to Data: Field Methods for Studying Ongoing Social Organizations.* Chicago: Aldine.

Halberstam, David. 1979. *The Powers That Be.* New York: Dell.

Halberstam, David. 1976a. "CBS: The Power and the Profits (Part I)." *Atlantic,* January, pp. 33–71.

Halberstam, David. 1976b. "CBS: The Power and the Profits (Part II)." *Atlantic,* February, pp. 52–91.

Halberstam, David. 1976c. "The Coming of Carter." *Newsweek,* July 19, p. 11.

Hanson, C. T. 1983. "Gunsmoke and Sleeping Dogs: The Prez's Press at Midterm." *Columbia Journalism Review,* May-June, pp. 26–36.

Hargrove, Erwin C. 1988. "Jimmy Carter: The Politics of Public Goods." In

Leadership in the Modern Presidency, ed. Fred I. Greenstein, pp. 228–59. Cambridge, MA: Harvard University Press.

Harney, Russell F., and Vernon A. Stone. 1969. "Television and Newspaper Front Page Coverage of a Major News Story." *Journal of Broadcasting* 13 (Spring): 181–88.

Hart, John. 1977. "A Picture of Expected Carter-Press Relations." *New York Times,* February 7, p. 23.

Herbers, John. 1976. *No Thank You, Mr. President.* New York: Norton.

Herbers, John. 1982. "The President and the Press Corps." *New York Times Magazine,* May 9, pp. 45–98.

Hertsgaard, Mark. 1988. *On Bended Knee: The Press and the Reagan Presidency.* New York: Farrar, Straus, Giroux.

Hess, Stephen. 1978. "The President and the Press: The Boredom Factor." *Washington Post,* May 13, p. A11.

Hess, Stephen. 1981. *The Washington Reporters.* Washington, DC: Brookings Institution.

Hess, Stephen. 1983. "The Golden Triangle: Press Relations at the White House, State Department, and Department of Defense." Paper presented at War, Peace and the News Media Conference, New York University School of Journalism, March 13–14.

Heumann, Joe. 1980. "U.S. Network Television: Melodrama and the Iranian Crisis." *Middle East Review,* Summer-Fall, pp. 51–55.

Hiebert, Ray E. 1966. *The Press in Washington.* New York: Dodd, Mead.

Hill, Frederic B. 1980. "Media Diplomacy." *Washington Journalism Review* 2:11.

Holmes, Deborah. 1986. *Governing the Press: Media Freedom in the U.S. and Great Britain.* Boulder, CO: Westview.

Hoyt, Ken, and Frances Spatz Leighton. 1980. *Drunk before Noon: The Behind the Scenes Story of the Washington Press Corps.* Englewood Cliffs, NJ: Prentice-Hall.

Hurewitz, J. C. 1980. "Another View of Iran and the Press." *Columbia Journalism Review,* May-June, pp. 19–21.

Iyengar, S.; Mark D. Peters; and Donald Kinder. 1982. "Experimental Demonstrations of the 'Not So Minimal' Consequences of Television News Progress." *American Political Science Review* 76, no. 4: 848–58.

Johnson, Haynes. 1980. *In the Absence of Power: Governing in America.* New York: Viking.

Johnson, John. 1976. *The News People.* Urbana, IL: University of Illinois Press.

Jordan, Hamilton. 1982. *Crisis: The Last Year of the Carter Presidency.* New York: G. P. Putnam's Sons.

Joseph, Ted. 1973. "How White House Correspondents Feel About Background Briefings." *Journalism Quarterly* 50: 509–16.

Joyce, Ed. 1988. *Prime Times, Bad Times.* New York: Doubleday.

Juergens, George. 1981. *News from the White House: The Presidential-Press Relationship in the Progressive Era.* Chicago: University of Chicago Press.

Kalb, Marvin, and Frederick Mayer. 1988. "Reviving the Presidential News Conference: A Report of the Harvard Commission on the Presidential

News Conference." Joan Shorenstein Barone Center on the Press, Politics, and Public Policy, John F. Kennedy School of Government, Harvard University. Mimeograph.

Karl, Patricia A. 1982. "Media Diplomacy." In *The Communications Revolution in Politics*, ed. Gerald Benjamin, Proceedings of the Academy of Political Science 34, no. 4: New York: Academy of Political Science, pp. 143–152.

Karp, Walter. 1985. "Liberty under Siege: The Reagan Administration's Taste for Autocracy." *Harper's*, November, pp. 53–67.

Keebler, Nancy. 1986. "Iran: It Was a Textbook Case But the Lessons Remain Unclear." *Encore Magazine* (*Sacramento Bee* supplement), January 19, p. 5.

Kenski, Henry C. 1977. "Inflation and Presidential Popularity." *Public Opinion Quarterly* 41 (Spring): 86–90.

Keogh, James. 1972. *President Nixon and the Press*. New York: Funk and Wagnalls.

Kernell, Samuel. 1977. "Presidential Popularity and Negative Voting: An Alternative Explanation of the Midterm Congressional Decline of the President's Party." *American Political Science Review* 71 (March): 44–46.

Kernell, Samuel. 1978. "Explaining Presidential Popularity: How Ad Hoc Theorizing, Misplaced Emphasis, and Insufficient Care in Measuring One's Variables Refuted Common Sense and Led Conventional Wisdom Down the Path of Anomalies." *American Political Science Review* 72 (June): 506–22.

Kernell, Samuel, and Peter W. Sperlich. 1975. "Public Support for Presidents." In *Perspectives on the Presidency*, ed. Aaron Wildavsky, pp. 141–81. Boston: Little, Brown.

Kessel, John H. 1977. "Seasons of Presidential Politics." *Social Science Quarterly* 58: 418–35.

Kinsley, Michael. 1986. "The Case for Glee (Watching Ronald Reagan's Fall from Popularity)." *Washington Post*, December 4, p. A23.

Kirschten, Dick. 1981. "Life in the White House Fishbowl—Brady Takes Charge as Press Chief." *National Journal*, January 31, p. 180.

Kirschten, Dick. 1984. "Communications Reshuffling Intended to Help Reagan Do What He Does Best." *National Journal*, January 28, pp. 153–57.

Klein, Herbert G. 1980. *Making It Perfectly Clear*. Garden City: Doubleday.

Kranz, Harry. 1975. "The Presidency and the Press—Who Is Right?" In *Perspectives on the Presidency*, ed. Aaron Wildavsky, pp. 205–20. Boston: Little, Brown.

Kumar, Martha J., and Michael Grossman. 1982. "Images of the White House in the Media." In *The President and the Public*, ed. Doris A. Graber, pp. 85–110. Philadelphia: Institute for the Study of Human Issues.

Lee, Richard E., ed. 1970. *Politics and the Press*. Washington, DC: Acropolis Books.

Leviero, Anthony. 1950. "Truman Defends Private Interview in a Spirited Session with Press." *New York Times*, February 17, p. 2.

"Lie of the Week." 1941. *Time*, September 8, p. 10.

Lippmann, Walter. 1922. *Public Opinion*. New York: Free Press.

Locander, Robert. 1978. "The President, the Press, and the Public: Friends and Enemies of Democracy." *Presidential Studies Quarterly* 8, no. 2 (Spring): 130–50.

Locander, Robert. 1979. "The Adversary Relationship: A New Look at an Old Idea." *Presidential Studies Quarterly* 9 (Summer): 266–74.

Locander, Robert. 1980. "Carter and the Press: The First Two Years." *Presidential Studies Quarterly* 10 (Winter): 106–20.

Lofland, John, and Lynn H. Lofland. 1984. *Analyzing Social Settings*. 2nd ed. Salt Lake City: Wadsworth.

Lowry, Dennis T. 1971a. "Agnew and the Network News: A Before/After Content Analysis." *Journalism Quarterly* 53 (Summer): 205–10.

Lowry, Dennis T. 1971b. "Gresham's Law and Network T.V. News Selection." *Journal of Broadcasting* 15 (Fall): 397–409.

Mackuen, Michael Bruce. 1981. *More Than News: Media Power in Public Affairs*. Beverly Hills, CA: Sage.

MacNeil, Robert. 1968. *The People Machines: The Influences of Television on American Politics*. New York: Harper & Row.

Manheim, Jarol B., and William Lammers. 1981. "The News Conference and Presidential Leadership of Public Opinion: Does the Tail Wag the Dog?" *Presidential Studies Quarterly* 11 (Spring): 177–88.

Marbut, F. B. 1971. *New from the Capital*. Carbondale, Illinois: Southern Illinois University Press.

Mayer, Martin. 1972. *About Television*. New York: Harper & Row.

McCartney, James. 1977. "The Triumph of Junk News." *Columbia Journalism Review*, January-February, pp. 17–21.

McLuhan, Marshall. 1964. *Understanding Media*. New York: Signet.

McManus, Doyle. 1987. "Dateline Washington: *Gipperdemmerung*." *Foreign Policy* 66: 156–72.

Meer, Jeffrey. 1986. "Reagan's Facial Teflon." *Psychology Today*, January, p. 18.

Meeseke, Milan D., and Mohamad Hamid Javaheri. 1982. "Network Television Coverage of the Iranian Hostage Crisis." *Journalism Quarterly* 59: 641–45.

"Meeting the Press: A Conversation with David Gergen and Jody Powell." 1982. *Public Opinion*, December-January, pp. 10–11, 57.

Merrill, John C. 1965. "How *Time* Stereotyped Three U.S. Presidents." *Journalism Quarterly* 42 (Autumn): 563–70.

Metz, Robert. 1975. *CBS: Reflections in a Bloodshot Eye*. New York: New American Library.

Mickeleson, Sig. 1972. *The Electric Mirror*. New York: Dodd, Mead.

Minow, Newton N.; John B. Martin; and Lee M. Mitchell. 1973. *Presidential Television*. New York: Basic Books.

Morgan, David. 1978. *The Capital Press Corps: Newsmen and the Governing of New York State*. New York: Greenwood Press.

Morgan, E. P.; M. Ways; C. Mollenhoff; P. Lisagor; and H. G. Klein. 1971. *The Presidency and the Press Conference*. Washington, DC: American Enterprise Institute for Public Policy Research.

Morgenstern, Steven, ed. 1979. *Inside the TV Business*. New York: Sterling.

Mosettig, Michael D. 1981. "The Revolution in Communications and Diplomacy." *Academy of Political Science Proceedings* 35: 190–201.

Mott, Frank Luther. 1978. *American Journalism: A History, 1690–1960.* 3d ed. New York: Greenwood Press.

Moyers, Bill. 1986. "Taking CBS News to Task." *Newsweek,* September 15, p. 53.

Moynihan, Daniel P. 1975. "The Presidency and the Press." In *Perspectives on the Presidency,* ed. Aaron Wildavsky, pp. 184–205. Boston: Little, Brown.

Muller, John E. 1973. *War, Presidents and Public Opinion.* New York: John Wiley and Sons.

Nessen, Ron. 1978a. *It Sure Looks Different from the Inside.* Chicago: Playboy Press.

Nessen, Ron. 1978b. "Saving the Worst Till Last." *TV Guide,* February 16, pp. 5–8.

Nessen, Ron. 1980. "The Washington You Can't See on Television." *TV Guide,* September 20, pp. 9–12.

Neustadt, Richard E. 1980. *Presidential Power: The Politics of Leadership from FDR to Carter.* New York: John Wiley and Sons.

Nimmo, Dan. 1963. *Newsgathering in Washington.* New York: Atherton Press.

Nimmo, Dan. 1970. *The Political Persuaders.* Englewood Cliffs, NJ: Prentice-Hall.

Nimmo, Dan, and James E. Combs. 1985. *Nightly Horrors: Crisis Coverage by Television Network News.* Knoxville: University of Tennessee Press.

Oberdorfer, Don. 1981. "Now That It's Over the Press Needs to Reflect on Its Role." *Washington Journalism Review* 3:37–38.

O'Keefe, Garrett J. 1980. "Political Malaise and Reliance on Media: TV and Newspaper Reliance Produce Integrative Political Attitudes." *Journalism Quarterly* 57 (Spring): 122–28.

Osborne, Trudi. 1977. "The White House Press Corps: Let AP Cover the Assassinations." *Washington Monthly* 8 (February): 16–24.

Palentz, David L., and Martha Elson. 1976. "Television Coverage of Presidential Conventions: Now You See It, Now You Don't." *Political Science Quarterly* 91 (Spring): 109–31.

Palentz, David L., and K. Kendall Guthrie. 1985. "Three-Faced Ronald Reagan." Unpublished paper, Duke University.

Palentz, David L., and Roberta Pearson. 1978. "The Way You Look Tonight: A Critique of Television News Criticism." In *Television Network News: Issues in Content Research,* ed. William C. Adams and Fay Schreibaum. Washington, DC: School of International Affairs, George Washington University.

Palentz, David L., and Richard J. Vinegar. 1977–78. "Presidents on Television: Effects of Instant Analysis." *Public Opinion Quarterly* 41 (Winter): 488–97.

Patterson, Thomas E. 1980. *The Mass Media Election.* New York: Praeger.

Patterson, Thomas E., and Robert D. McClure. 1976. *The Unseeing Eye: The Myth of Television Power in National Elections.* New York: G. P. Putnam's Sons.

Pear, Robert. 1987. "Missing the Iran Arms Story: Did the Press Fail?" *New York Times*, March 4, p. A15.

Pearce, Alan. 1987. *NBC News Division: The Economics of Prime Time Access*. New York: Arno Press.

Peters, Charles. 1973. "Why the White House Press Didn't Get the Watergate Story." *Washington Monthly*, July-August, pp. 7–15.

Pierpoint, Robert. 1981. *At the White House*. New York: G. P. Putnam's Sons.

Pincus, Walter. 1971. "Before the Pentagon Papers: Why the Press Failed." *New York* 4, no. 39 (June 19): 36.

Pollard, James E. 1964. *The President and the Press: Truman to Johnson*. Washington, DC: Public Affairs Press.

Pollard, James E. 1973. *The President and the Press*. New York: Octagon Books.

Porter, William E. 1976. *Assault on the Media*. Ann Arbor: University of Michigan Press.

Powell, Jody. 1984. *The Other Side of the Story*. New York: William Morrow.

Powers, Ron. 1978. *The Newscasters: The News Business as Show Business*. New York: St. Martin's Press.

Purvis, Hoyt, ed. 1976. *The Presidency and the Press*. Austin: University of Texas Press. Proceedings of a colloquium on presidential-press relations at the Lyndon B. Johnson School of Public and Environmental Affairs.

Randolph, Eleanor. 1978. "The Secret Pleasures of the White House Press." *Washington Monthly*, March, pp. 29–35.

Randolph, Eleanor. 1987. "How News Hounds Blew the Iran-Contra Story." *Washington Post*, November 15, p. C1–C4.

Ranney, Austin. 1983. *Channels of Power*. New York: Basic Books.

Raphel, Arnold. 1981–82. *Media Coverage of the Hostage Negotiations—From Fact to Fiction*. Executive Seminar in National and International Affairs, 24th Session. U.S. Department of State. Foreign Service Institute.

Rather, Dan. 1976. Quoted in *The Presidency and the Press*, ed. Hoyt Purvis. Austin: University of Texas Press. Proceedings of a colloquium on presidential-press relations at the Lyndon B. Johnson School of Public and Environmental Affairs.

Rather, Dan. 1977. *The Camera Never Blinks*. New York: Morrow.

Rather, Dan. 1987. "From Murrow to Mediocrity?" *New York Times*, March 10, p. 25.

Reasoner, Harry. 1977. *Before the Colors Fade*. New York: Morrow.

Reedy, George. 1970. *The Twilight of the Presidency*. New York: World Publishing.

Reedy, George. 1976. "The President and the Press: Struggle for Dominance." *Annals of the Academy of Political and Social Science* 427: 65–72.

Reel, Frank A. 1979. *The Networks: How They Stole the Show*. New York: Charles Scribner's Sons.

Regan, Donald T. 1988. *For the Record*. New York: Harcourt.

"Report of the Commission on Presidential Press Conferences." 1980. White Burkett Miller Center of Public Affairs, University of Virginia. Washington, DC: University Press of America.

Rivers, William E. 1962. "The Correspondents after 25 Years." *Columbia Journalism Review* 1 (Spring): 5.

Rivers, William E. 1970. *The Adversaries: Politics and the Press*. Boston: Beacon Press.

Rivers, William E.; Theodore Peterson; and Jay W. Jense. 1971. *The Mass Media and Modern Society*. 2d ed. San Francisco: Rinehart Press.

Robinson, John B., and Mark R. Levy. 1986. *The Main Source: Learning from T.V. News*. Beverly Hills: Sage.

Robinson, Michael J. 1971. "The Audience for National TV News Programs." *Public Opinion Quarterly* 35 (Fall): 403–05.

Robinson, Michael J. 1977. "Television and American Politics: 1956–1976." *Public Interest*, (Spring): 3–39.

Robinson, Michael J., and Kevin R. Appel. 1979. "Network News Coverage of Congress." *Political Science Quarterly* 94, no. 3 (Fall): 407–18.

Robinson, Michael J., and Margaret A. Sheehan. 1983. *Over the Wire and on T.V.* New York: Sage.

Roosevelt, Franklin D. 1972. *Complete Presidential Press Conferences of Franklin Roosevelt*. Volumes 15–16. 1940. Introduction by Jonathan Daniels. New York: Da Capo Press.

Roper, B. 1969. "A Ten Year Study of Public Attitudes toward Television and Other Mass Media, 1959–1968." New York: Television Information Office.

Rosenstiel, Thomas B. 1989. "The Media: Bush Plays it Cozy." *Los Angeles Times*, December 9, p. 1t.

Rosenstiel, Thomas B., and James Gerstenzang. 1989. "Image: Bush's Neighborly Style Brings Risk in Television Age." *Los Angeles Times*, April 30, Part I, p. 28.

Rosten, Leo. 1937. *The Washington Correspondents*. New York: Harcourt.

Russo, Frank. 1971–72. "A Study of Bias in TV Coverage of the Vietnam War: 1969 and 1970." *Public Opinion Quarterly* 35 (Winter): 539–43.

Said, E. W. 1981. "Inside Islam." *Harper's*, January, pp. 25–32.

Salinger, Pierre. 1981. *America Held Hostage: The Secret Negotiations*. Garden City, NY: Doubleday.

Santini, Maureen. 1983. "Reagan's Call for Good News on T.V. is Rejected by Networks as a Ploy." *Courier Journal* (Louisville, KY), March 4, p. A4.

Sauter, Van Gordon. 1988. "A Real Barroom Brawl Enlivens Primary Season, But Don't Bet on a Rerun." *Los Angeles Times*, January 29, p. 7.

Savitch, Jessica. 1982. *Anchorwoman*. New York: Putnam and Sons.

Schardt, Arlie. 1979. "Dateline Teheran." *Newsweek*, December 3, p. 87.

Schlesinger, Arthur M., Jr. 1973. *The Imperial Presidency*. Boston: Houghton-Mifflin.

Schorr, Daniel. 1977. *Clearing the Air*. Boston: Houghton-Mifflin.

Schudson, Michael. 1982. "The Politics of the Narrative Form: The Emergence of News Conventions in Print and Television." *Daedalus*, (Fall), pp. 97–112.

Schumacher, F. Carl, and George C. Wilson. 1971. *Bridge of No Return*. New York: Harcourt.

Shabecoff, Philip G. 1983. "Watt Battled Rising Tide." *New York Times,* October 10, pp. 1.

Shaffir, William B.; Robert A. Stebbins; and Allan Turowetz. 1980. *Fieldwork Experience: Qualitative Approaches to Social Research.* New York: St. Martin's Press.

Sharpe, Kenneth E. 1987. "The Real Cause of Irangate." *Foreign Policy* 68 (Fall): 19–41.

Shaw, Donald L., and Maxwell E. McCombs, eds. 1977. *The Emergence of Political Issues: The Agenda Setting Function of the Press.* St. Paul, MN: West.

Sickels, Robert J. 1974. *Presidential Transactions.* Englewood Cliffs, NJ: Prentice-Hall.

Siebert, Leon. 1978. "Newsmen and Campaigners: Organization Men Make the News." *Political Science Quarterly* 93, no. 3: 465–70.

Sigal, Leon V. 1973. *Reporters and Officials: The Organization and Politics of Newsmaking.* Lexington, MA: D. C. Heath.

Sigelman, Lee. 1973. "Reporting the News: An Organizational Analysis." *American Journal of Sociology* 79, no. 1: 132–51.

Sigelman, Lee. 1979. "The Dynamics of Presidential Support: An Overview of Research Findings." *Presidential Studies Quarterly* 2 (Spring): 206–16.

Small, William J. 1970. *To Kill a Messenger.* New York: Hastings House.

Small, William J. 1972. *Political Power and the Press.* New York: W. W. Norton.

Smith, Gaddis. 1986. *Morality, Reason, and Power: American Diplomacy in the Carter Years.* New York: Hill and Wang.

Smith, Hedrick. 1981. "Blunt and Simple: Reagan's Style Evokes Fireside Chat But with Visual Aids and No Cardigan." *New York Times,* February 7, p. 23.

Smoller, Fredric T. 1986. "The Six O'Clock Presidency: Patterns of Network News Coverage of the President." *Presidential Studies Quarterly* 16: 31–49.

Smoller, Fredric T. 1988. "Presidents and Their Critics." *Congress and the Presidency* 15, no. 1 (Spring): 75–89.

Smoller, Fredric T., and Keith Fitzgerald. 1981. "Cities Evaluate the President: A Focus Group Discussion of the Carter and Reagan Presidencies." Unpublished Paper, Department of Political Science, Indiana University, Bloomington, Indiana.

Speakes, Larry. 1988. *Speaking Out.* New York: Charles Scribner's.

Speakes, Larry. 1983. "Speakes Says Media Are Blind to Silver Lining." *Broadcasting,* February 7, p. 36.

Spragens, William C. 1980. *From Spokesman to Press Secretary.* Washington, DC: University Press of America.

Spragens, William C. 1979. *The Presidency and the Mass Media in the Age of Television.* Washington, DC: University Press of America.

Stein, Herbert. 1975. "Media Distortions: A Former Official's View." *Columbia Journalism Review,* March-April, p. 40.

Stein, M. L. 1987. "Missing the Big One." *Editor and Publisher,* July 11, p. 10.

Stevenson, Robert L.; Richard A. Eisenger; Barry M. Feinberg; and Alan B.

Kotok. 1973. "Untwisting the 'Newstwisters': A Replication of Efron's Study." *Journalism Quarterly* 50 (Summer): 211–19.

Stimson, James A. 1976. "Public Support for American Presidents: A Cyclical Model." *Public Opinion Quarterly* 40 (Spring): 1–21.

Stimson, James A. 1976–77. "On Disillusionment with the Expectation/ Disillusion Theory: A Rejoinder." *Public Opinion Quarterly* 40 (Winter): 541–43.

Strouse, James G. 1975. *The Mass Media, Public Opinion, and Public Policy Analysis.* Columbus, OH: Charles E. Merrill.

Talese, Gay. 1970. *The Kingdom and the Power.* New York: Bantam.

"The Tattletale White House." 1980. *Newsweek,* February 25, p. 21.

Tebbel, John. 1974. *The Media in America.* New York: Crowell.

Tebbel, John, and Sarah Miles Watts. 1985. *The Press and the Presidency.* New York: Oxford.

"Television's Blinding Power." 1987. *U.S. News & World Report,* July 27, pp. 18–21.

Thomas, Helen. 1975. *Dateline: White House.* New York: Macmillan.

Thompson, Denneth W., ed. 1983. *Ten Presidents and the Press.* Washington, DC: University Press of America.

The Tower Commission Report. 1987. New York: Bantam Books.

"Transcript of President's Address Defining His Proposals on Budget for 1983." 1982. *New York Times,* April 30, p. A16.

Tuchman, Gaye. 1974. *The TV Establishment.* Englewood Cliffs, NJ: Prentice-Hall.

Tuchman, Gaye. 1978. *Making the News: A Study in the Construction of Reality.* New York: Free Press.

Tuchman, Gaye. 1973a. "Making News by Doing Work: Routinizing the Unexpected." *American Journal of Sociology* 79 (July): 110–31.

Tuchman, Gaye. 1973b. "The Technology of Objectivity: Doing 'Objective' TV News Film." *Urban Life and Culture* 2 (April): 3–26.

Tuchman, Gaye. 1975. "Determinants of the Outcomes of Midterm Congressional Elections." *American Political Science Review* 69 (September): 812–26.

Tumstall, Jeremy. 1971. *Journalists at Work.* Beverly Hills, CA: Sage.

"TV's Controversial Role in the Iran Crisis." 1979. *U.S. News & World Report,* December 24, p. 7.

Ungar, Stanford J. 1977. "By Trivia Obsessed." *Columbia Journalism Review* 16 (January-February): 16–17.

United States. National Archives. 1965. *Public Papers of the Presidents: Harry Truman, January 1 to December 31, 1950.* Washington, DC: Government Printing Office.

Von Hoffman, Nicholas. 1980a. "ABC Held Hostage." *New Republic,* May 10, pp. 15–17.

Von Hoffman, Nicholas. 1980b. "Hodding Carter Tells (Almost) All." *Columbia Journalism Review,* November-December, pp. 36–37.

Wald, Matthew. 1987. "Reagan Staff Depicted as Failing Him." *New York Times,* March 4, p. A15.

"Washington Press Corps." 1981. *Newsweek,* May 25, p. 90.

"The Way It Is for Network News." 1987. *U.S. News & World Report,* March 16, pp. 51–54.

Watt, James G. 1985. The Courage of a Conservative. New York: Simon and Schuster.

Wayne, Steven J. 1978. *The Legislative Presidency.* New York: Harper & Row.

Weaver, Paul H. 1972. "Is Television News Biased?" *Public Interest* 26 (Winter): 57–74.

Weaver, Paul H. 1976. "Captives of Melodrama." *New York Times Magazine,* August 29, pp. 6–58.

Weisman, John. 1983. "Who's Toughest on the White House—and Why." *TV Guide.* pp. 4–15.

Weisman, Steven R. 1984. "The President and the Press: The Art of Controlled Access." *New York Times Magazine,* October 14, pp. 34–83.

"What the Press Must Do." 1974. *Newsweek,* December 9, p. 15.

White, Theodore H. 1961. *The Making of the President 1960.* New York: Atheneum.

"White House Pillars: Is Democracy Made for TV?" 1980. *Commonweal* 107 (July 4): 404.

Whiteside, Thomas. 1975. "Annals of Television: Shaking the Tree." *New Yorker,* March 17, p. 84.

Wicker, Tom. 1979. *On Press.* New York: Berkeley Books.

Wildavsky, Aaron, ed. 1975. *Perspectives on the Presidency.* Boston: Little, Brown.

Will, George F. 1983. "Television and Image Tuners." *Newsweek,* February 14, p. 83.

Wisehart, Bob. 1986. "The Story That Changed TV News—Forever." *Encore Magazine* (Sacramento Bee supplement), January 19, p. 4.

Witcover, Jules. 1973. "How Well Does the White House Press Perform?" *Columbia Journalism Review,* November-December, pp. 39–43.

Witcover, Jules. 1977a. *Marathon.* New York: Viking.

Witcover, Jules. 1977b. *Marathon: The Pursuit of the Presidency, 1972–1976.* New York: New American Library.

Wolfson, Lewis W. 1975. "A Report on the State of the Presidential Press Conference." New York: The National News Council.

Woodruff, Judy. 1982. *This Is Judy Woodruff at the White House.* Reading, MA: Addison-Wesley.

Woodward, Bob, and Carl Bernstein. 1976. *The Final Days.* New York: Simon and Schuster.

Wooten, James. 1977. "Carter's Style: Making Aides Apprehensive." *New York Times,* April 25, p. 1t.

Wooten, James. 1979. "Can Rafshooning Save Jimmy Carter?" *Esquire,* March, pp. 25–33.

The World Almanac and Book of Facts. 1989. New York: Scripps Howard.

Zufkin, Cliff. 1981. "Mass Communications and Public Opinion." In *Handbook of Political Communications,* ed. Dan Nimmo and Keith R. Sanders, pp. 359–90. Beverly Hills, CA: Sage.

Index

ABOUT THE AUTHOR

FREDRIC T. SMOLLER received his Ph.D. from Indiana University. He is currently an Associate Professor of political science at Chapman College, where he teaches courses on American politics. His articles have appeared in *Presidential Studies Quarterly, Congress and the Presidency,* and *The Political Science Teacher.*